IS
THAT
MOTHER
IN
THE
BOTTLE?

IS
THAT
MOTHER
IN
THE
BOTTLE?

WHERE LANGUAGE CAME FROM
AND WHERE IT IS GOING

by

JESSICA
DAVIDSON

FRANKLIN WATTS, INC. · NEW YORK · 1972

Library of Congress Cataloging in Publication Data

Davidson, Jessica.
    Is that mother in the bottle?

    SUMMARY: Examines the ways language
grows and changes and the effect of different syntax
and speech patterns on communication.
    1. Linguistics–Juvenile literature. [1. Linguis-
tics] I. Title.
P124.D35   410   72-1997
ISBN 0-531-02575-6

For Jean Mann
who speaks my language

Previous Books by the Author

Mind in a Maze (with William G. Martin)
What I Tell You Three Times Is True
The Square Root of Tuesday

CONTENTS

IS
THAT
MOTHER
IN
THE
BOTTLE?

CHAPTER I

Do You See What I Mean?

Anyone who has walked the streets of New York at one end of a leash knows what a wealth of signposts there are that use neither words nor pictures to communicate. Every hydrant, every lamppost, every spindly tree trunk in its little fenced-in square of ground is covered with information that can be read by the nose on the head at the other end of the leash. Dogs, wolves, cats, and many other creatures stake out a territory and leave signs for others of their kind to read by their sense of smell.

A bee leaves the hive to search for nectar. When it finds some, it returns to the hive to tell the other bees where it is. To do so, the bee uses neither words nor sounds, and yet it can communicate not only where the nectar is but what kind it is. The bee performs a dance at the hive, waggling and turning in figure eights. The direction it's headed in when it waggles—toward or away from or at an angle to the sun—indicates the direction of the nectar from the hive, while the speed of its dance—the number of turns it makes in a minute—indicates the distance of the nectar from the hive. The information given by the dance is accurate and reliable, and the bees in the hive understand and act upon the information.

Cats' and dogs' tails are very expressive instruments. People accustomed to dogs and unacquainted with cats are in for a surprise if they assume that a cat's wagging tail means the same as a dog's. A cat's twitching tail can almost always be interpreted to mean, "Leave me alone; if you don't, you'll be sorry." Even among dogs, a wagging tail is not always a sign of joy and happy greeting. If a male dog approaches another with his tail held high and wagging slowly, it is a sign to the second dog that he considers himself to be the top dog. If both male dogs approach each other in this way, a fight will often follow, to establish which claim to mastery is correct. If, on the other hand, the wagging tail is low and rapid, the dog is admitting that he's licked before the fight starts, and the top dog need not prove his claim. In just this way, when a dog that has been punished by his human master comes up to him in a crouched position with his tail wagging fast between his legs, he is saying quite clearly, "I'm sorry; I won't do it again; you're the boss." He is not necessarily saying, "I'm happy and I love you."

Watching the bee, the dog, the cat, it would be quite correct for us to say, "I *see* what you mean." People also have many ways of communicating feelings and ideas without the use of sounds of any kind. How many times have you bought a candy bar just by pointing to the one you wanted, giving the storekeeper some money, getting change, and all the while not saying, not needing to say a word?

In a perfectly ordinary everyday way without words or sounds, it is quite easy to say any of the following:

I don't want any.
I love you.
I hate you.
Go away!
Stop!
Come here.
You disgust me.
Phooey on you!
I'm helpless.
I'm sorry for you.
That's delicious.
I'm afraid of you.
I don't believe it.
I agree.
That hurts!
I don't know.
Maybe.
I'll be glad to help you.
I'm bored.
It's too hot.
It's too cold.
Open it.
Close it.

With a shrug of the shoulders or a raised eyebrow, you can express a variety of feelings and reactions. Anyone watching you will see what you mean. There is communication, but is it a language? "Any means of expressing ideas or emotions" is one definition of language the dictionary offers. Such a definition is loose enough to include as language not only gestures and facial expressions but even the kind of clothes you wear, the length and style of your hair, your way of walking, the furnishings of your room, the pictures on your walls, the car your family drives, and the title of the books you're carrying. It would also include a dog's panting, your yawning, the chattering of your teeth. All these are expressions of ideas or emotions, and they can serve to communicate these ideas or emotions to others. But the trouble with considering these as language is that while a dog's panting signifies that he is hot, the dog is not panting in order to tell someone he is hot. He's panting because that's his way of cooling off. You don't yawn to announce that you're sleepy, nor do your teeth chatter to communicate the fact that you're cold. The definition is too loose.

Let's say at least that for something to qualify as a language, there must be sound, and that the sound must be made on purpose. What kind of sound? Consider this conversation:

"Apso zolopar dra flinsk."

"What did you say?"

"Apso zolopar dra flinsk."

"What are you talking about? I don't get it."

"Well, of course not. You don't know the language."

"What language?"

"My private language. The one I'm inventing."

"Well, what does apso—whatever you said—mean?"

"I said it was my *private* language. So, naturally, I'm not going to tell you what it means."

"Who else knows this language?"

"Nobody, stupid. I told you it's my *private* language. I'm the only one who knows how to speak it."

"Oh, well, in that case—nam venoblat taga gralemsteel."

"What was *that?*"

"*My* private language."

This conversation is going nowhere. To speak a language that no one else understands is to have a seesaw with no one to sit on the opposite end. You can bounce up and down a little bit, but it's not much fun. Language is for communication between at least two people and usually a great many more. If nobody whatever understands the sounds, they are no more than interesting noises.

If you've taught a parrot to speak, you can understand what it says, but since the parrot does not understand it, there's no communication. Just as parrots and parrakeets can learn to imitate human speech, so some people are good at imitating bird whistles and can even manage to carry on what sounds like a conversation with a crow or a cardinal. But since they no more understand what they're whistling than the parrot understands what it says, there's no language involved, any more than there is with *apso zolopar*. Imitation of bird sounds has been put to very good use. When a small town in Pennsylvania was plagued by the presence of thousands of starlings, a professor at the state university had the idea of tape-recording the sounds made by a starling shrieking in terror when it was caught. He then played back the tape at high volume all over the town whenever the starlings were roosting. They left.

The sounds the professor played were intended to communicate, and they did so. But it was not he who was speaking. The situation is a little like that of a foreign official visiting a country whose language he does not speak. Someone writes a speech for him in the language and teaches him how to pronounce the words, and he does so. If he pronounces the sounds reasonably well, his audience will understand and applaud. He has communicated though he has not understood a single word of his own speech. He is simply parroting.

Language is sound that goes two ways. What you say to me in a language, I can hear and say back to you. When you whistle to your dog and he comes to your call barking happily, no conversation has taken place, and no language has been used because, although you're communicating with him, he can't whistle back at you and your barking's a poor imitation of what you hear.

After many years of trying to teach the human language to animals, a few experimenters have succeeded in very limited ways, but it is still not clear just how much the animals really understand of the language they are hearing and repeating. The couple who tried to bring up a chimpanzee baby as they would a child managed to teach it to say three words: *name, papa,* and *cup,* but no more. Dr. Joseph Lilly has been teaching dolphins English with some minor success, and Elisabeth Mann Borgese has developed a typewriter on which her dog can type what, now and then, turns out to be more or less readable English. An example: GOOD DG DOG GO BED. But these experiments are still a long way from proving that it is possible for humans and animals to speak English together and really say anything.

But if animals and man cannot communicate with each other, can animals nevertheless be said to have a language of their own? Are the barks and grunts and moos and purrs and cock-a-doodle-doos languages? Certainly, to some extent, these sounds communicate ideas and emotions within the species. They tell of the presence of food or of danger. They tell of pleasure, of contentment, of pain, of fear. There are elaborate courtship and mating calls. There are birdsongs to indicate defense of territory. Animals can understand human speech in these terms. A command to lie down, to heel, to sit, is a kind of human bark a dog can learn as readily as you can learn to distinguish your dog's bark-to-announce-a-visitor from his yelp of pain.

People make sounds of this kind to each other as well—hisses, whistles, sharp intakes of breath, clicks of the tongue and snaps of the fingers, stamping, banging, and shrieking all communicate clearly. Some of the words people use are sounds of this kind—"Ouch!" "Watch out!" "Hi there!" and "Darling!" If you were to *read* these words in a foreign language, it is quite likely that you would not understand them. (Which of them, for example, do you think *"Achtung!"* means? And which one is *"Schatz!"?*) But if you heard them shouted in the appropriate moment, you wouldn't have the slightest doubt as to their meaning. *"Ach-*

(9)

tung!" would be clearly understood to mean "Watch out!" and, in the right moment, you would believe that *"Schatz!"* really does mean "Darling!"

Are these signal noises language? If they are, then what about the mechanical noises man makes that are also intended to communicate information? The bugler blows reveille, calling everyone to wake up. Is this bugle call language? Is the alarm clock talking to you when it wakes you up in the morning? Certainly it is a sound that is intended to convey—and does convey—information.

If these sounds do not make a language, what's missing?

The two most important requirements have not yet been mentioned. For a language to be large enough to be useful, there must be the kind of flexibility that allows small bits of sound—letter sounds and syllables—to be combined in different ways to produce different meanings—*apt, tap,* and *pat,* for example. It must be possible for speaker and listener to distinguish closely related sounds like *bit* and *pit*. And with this flexibility there must be rules for making these combinations in such a way that it is possible to say things that have never been said before and that will yet be understood by those who speak the language and understand the rules. Chimpanzees are capable of making over forty different sounds, enough for a complicated language, but they do not have a language (as we are using the term). While they have an elaborate "vocabulary" of calls, each of these calls always means the same thing. They cannot be altered or combined to make new words to to convey new ideas. The apes can communicate the ideas of "come" and "danger" and "safe," but they cannot combine these to say, "If you come with me, I will keep you safe from danger."

No parrot has yet been found that can combine the words it knows into new sentences. The dog that understands "Come here" and "Don't" will not understand "Don't come here," much less, "You were supposed to come here but you didn't."

No matter how well you may communicate with your dog, no matter how well he understands that a leash in your hand means that you and he are going for a walk, or that a suitcase being packed indicates a journey, no matter how many commands to sit or heel or fetch he understands, there is no way for you to tell him, "I couldn't get you any hamburger today because the store was closed, but I'll definitely get some tomorrow." Nor is there any way for him to tell another dog that he didn't have his hamburger for dinner. Humans can speak and understand such language, but no nonhumans can. Except for the bee with its dancing, which describes a distant place, there is no creature other than man that has developed a way to talk about things that happened somewhere else at some other time, or that have never happened or that might happen in the future. And even the bee, if it does not find any nectar, does not return to the hive with a long story to excuse its failure.

The dancing of the bees is almost certainly controlled by heredity, as is the barking of the dog and the meowing of the cat. While some birds can learn the songs of other species, animals for the most part are controlled by heredity in the sounds they make. Humans, however, inherit not the knowledge of a language but the ability to learn language, much as they inherit the ability to breathe through lungs, not gills. A normal human child, no matter what his ancestry, will learn the language he hears spoken by the people around him. And his language is more than a series of cries and alarms. It can describe not only what he sees and feels but what he would like to see and feel, and what others have seen and dreamed of before he was born. His language can even be used—as here—to talk about how language came to be.

CHAPTER II

Can You Hear Me?

Primitive man certainly had at least as large an assortment of hoots and grunts and yelps as we find among the great apes today. But, as you've seen, these do not make a language. So how did language begin?

Nobody knows. But it is safe to say that no single person invented language. No one thought out a language with words like *apso zolopar* and then taught it to others. So we cannot look for the inventor of language as we might look for the inventor of the wheel or the safety pin.

Man's early ancestors inhabited various parts of the earth at least 1,750,000 years ago. Was he talking then? It is doubtful that we'll ever know the answer to this, but at least by the time, about fifty thousand years ago, when men were engaged in nomadic wandering in many parts of the world, language had certainly begun. People moving in groups together, chipping stones to make arrowheads and spearheads, hunting, skinning animals for clothing, sharing food, seeking shelter, making or preserving fire, must surely have spoken to one another.

Nobody knows just how it all began, but we can guess. Perhaps one day when a caveman had somehow become separated from his hunting group, he saw a huge and dangerous beast. He was about to give the danger cry when, for the first time, he stopped and thought. The beast was upwind of him and had not yet scented his presence. If he cried out so that his companions could hear the warning and run from the danger, the beast would hear him too, and he was closer to the beast than his companions were. Perhaps if he crept stealthily away he could do so unnoticed by the beast and have a head start on his flight back to the cave. Maybe he acted on this thought and gave the danger signal only when he had rejoined the group. And, having once used a danger cry as a way of *reporting* what he had seen earlier and at another place rather than as an immediate alarm, perhaps he tried it again. Perhaps others copied him.

Perhaps the earliest words came as commands in hunting or fighting. The cry that was ordinarily uttered by the chief of the group as he led the attack might then have been used as a signal to attack, uttered ahead of time, as a spur to his group. It could have been a question: Shall we attack?

Perhaps the need arose when a successful hunter came back to his cave with whatever he had found for his family. Making gestures and pointing, trying to describe how he had met his prey and conquered it, he began to repeat some of the cries of fear and of triumph to illustrate his pantomime. As we use pictures and gestures to enliven our word stories, perhaps early man used cries and grunts to enrich his pictures and gestures.

When you are making your way through a dark wood at night, it is reassuring to be in voice contact with friends you cannot see, even if you're not saying anything more than "Hi there!" or "How are you doing?" Perhaps at some time a hunting party was delayed and, finding their way back to their caves at night, they spoke in meaningless sounds to each other just to be sure they were all there together. And if the exchange of these meaningless sounds was reassuring, maybe the habit was established. Maybe the sounds later came to mean something, if only "Hi there! How're you doing?" and "Fine, thank you."

Once the idea of language had taken hold, what sort of sounds were used as words? There are lots of theories but none of them are very useful. One of the theories, for example, is known as the "bow-wow theory," according to which words were a sort of echo of sounds early man heard around him. There are words in all languages to support this theory—words like *coo* and *hiss* and *whirr* and *splash*. But no language has very many of these words. In any language most of the words are arbitrary sounds, sounds chosen without relation to the sound of the object or idea, chosen by agreement of the people who speak the language that this sound is the name by which the thing will be called, for no reason at all. Even the barks and grunts and whistles of animal calls meet this requirement.

The word *may* sound like the object or idea it symbolizes —words like *buzz* and *whirr* and *splash*—but it does not have to sound this way. A picture has to look like the object or idea it represents, but the word *tree* doesn't look like a tree and the word *argument* doesn't sound like an argument. A language could not be very useful if only those words could be used that were echoic—like echoes of the objects they symbolize. What words could then be found for house, sun, intelligence, beauty?

Even if words like *whirr* and *splash* were the very first words spoken, the bow-wow theory does not help to explain how other words like *dog* came into being, since a dog is not a bow-wow to anyone over two years old. And the echoic words are not the same in all languages. Some are so different from one another that they could as well have been made up without reference to the sound. Dogs, the world over, bark and yelp in pretty much the same way, but the Italians hear his bark as *bu-bu,* the French as *ouah-ouah,* the Germans as *hau-hau,* the Russians as *vaf-vaf* and the Chinese as *wang-wang.* Surely you could invent a word at least as good as *bow-wow* or *woof-woof* or any of the others. How about *hrok?*

Another theory is the "ding-dong theory," according to which there is some mystical connection between an object and its name: when a man saw a tree, for example, it set up a sort of bell ringing in his head and the sound that he heard was the name *tree.* This is not very far from the idea of the young children who told the psychologist Jean Piaget that the sun, the clouds, the mountains have always had their names and people could tell by looking at them what their names were. The early Greek philosopher Heraclitus thought that everything in the world had a name, as it has a color, a shape, a function, and that it was man's purpose to discover what these names were, just as it was his task to discover the laws of nature. The main difficulty with this theory is that, if it is true, there is only one correct language in the world. If the right name of dog is *dog,* then the Germans, who call it *Hund,* the French, who call it *chien,* the Spanish, who call it *perro,* and the Russians, who call it *sobaka,* are all mistaken. This theory might account for the reasons men gave for naming objects but it doesn't explain much about how language developed.

Then there is the "yo-he-ho theory," which says that man's first words were the grunts he made while lifting heavy objects or doing other work. This is perfectly possible, but then what were his second words? You are free to invent your own theory. No one really knows.

Apart from the question of how the first words were invented, what was language like in the Stone Age? You might think that because the way of life was so simple, language also was very uncomplicated, something like the "Me Tarzan, you Jane" of the Tarzan movies. But what evidence we have is against this.

African Bushmen and primitive tribes found in the interior of New Guinea speak highly complex languages. There are still Indians in Central America today who speak the languages of the Aztecs and Mayas. These languages and those of the North American Indians, which can still be studied as living languages, are very different in word and structure from those of Europe and Asia, but they are no simpler.

(17)

Quite recently a tiny tribe of a few dozen primitive people was found living under the triple canopy of a dense rain forest on the island of Mindanao in the Philippines. This tribe was called the Tasaday. They were stumbled upon when logging crews began to move into the area. Their life was so primitive that their clothing was made of palm leaves. Their tools were of stone, for they had not yet learned of metal. Their food was fish and small game they could trap and wild plants, for they had not yet learned to grow their own food. They had never left the forest because they did not know it was possible. There is as yet no way of knowing how long ago the Tasaday became separated from other tribes of the region but, judging by their way of life, one would suppose that the separation occurred during the Stone Age, which generally ended about six thousand years ago in this area. Yet the language of the Tasaday, far from being a simple group of names and action words, as one might suppose a Stone Age language would be, is a dialect of Manubo, a well-developed language spoken in the Philippines.

If the study of the languages of surviving primitive people does not help us to discover how language originated and developed, how are we going to find out? It may be that we will never know for certain, because the spoken language is nothing but wind blown in the air and, until modern devices like the tape recorder were invented, there was no way to catch this wind and hold it down for future study. Cave drawings, sculptures, pyramids, and many kinds of artifacts remain to be unearthed after thousands of years, but until language was written down there was no way to recapture it. The first recorded language was in the form of pictographs, which set down ideas, not sounds. Not until these pictographs developed to the point where they were used as rebuses (to represent syllables) like those in puzzles you find today

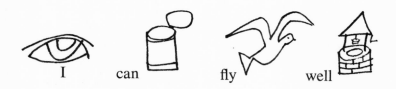

I   can   fly   well

are they useful for discovering what the spoken language was like. The first alphabet language, with letters representing sounds, dates back less than four thousand years. By this time men had settled as farmers and city dwellers in many parts of the world and spoke many different languages.

Today there are known to be somewhere between twenty-five hundred and thirty-five hundred languages, living and dead. It is hard to count them exactly because over two thousand of them are spoken by very few people (hundreds or a few thousands) and, while they seem to be languages on their own, it is possible that some are simply dialects of older languages. Even in well-established languages spoken and written by many people, it is difficult to decide how many there are. English as it is spoken and written today does not bear a very close resemblance to Old English of the Anglo-Saxon period or to the Middle English of the period between Old English and Modern English. Is En-

(19)

glish to be counted as one language, as three, or as more than three?

For people who are fond of precise numbers (even when they're known to be inaccurate) there is the figure of 2,796 languages that the French Academy has counted. Of these, there are only about one hundred and fifty languages that have a million or more speakers and only thirteen languages that are spoken by as many as fifty million each.*

How did there get to be so many languages? Was there ever a time when everyone spoke just one language? How do linguists hope to fill in the gap of the many thousands of years between the time when cavemen first spoke to each other and the time, about 1800 B.C., when the *sounds* of language were first recorded, in the Semitic languages and later in Sanskrit?

Linguists try to work the problem backwards. They start with what they have, the languages that exist today and are spoken all over the world and the earlier languages of which written records remain. They try to find similarities among them that would indicate a common ancestry. So far, no one has been able to prove that there was once just a single language; there may have been as many as twenty-five or thirty or even more. And this is not surprising because we still don't know whether man originated in just one place on earth, or how long he has been on earth, or how many places he wandered to before language began.

* These are: Chinese, English, Hindustani (in India and West Pakistan), Russian, Spanish (in Spain and in all of Latin America except Brazil), German, Japanese, Arabic, Bengali (in India and Bangladesh), Portuguese (in Portugal and Brazil), Indonesian, French, and Italian.

CHAPTER III

Family Trees

Suppose you've just met someone and you'd like to discover whether you are related to him. One easy solution is to say, "Yes, of course we're related. All of us can say we are sons of Adam, descendants of the first man, whoever he may have been and wherever he may have lived." But usually we look for more recent and more definite information. Are you, for example, personally related to King David of the Bible? Can you be sure, one way or the other? Most people know who their grandfathers were. Some, not many, can trace their ancestry back for several hundred years. Nobody can trace it back with any certainty for several thousands of years. But, in trying to find out if you and your new acquaintance are related, you go back as far as you can or need to.*

---

* You and your acquaintance will try to find a common ancestor among the ones you can identify.

The ancestry of a language differs from that of a person in that no special number of parents or grandparents is needed. A language may have a single parent or several. But there are families of languages as there are families of people. If several languages have a large number of words that are similar and if they have systems of grammar that are alike, they are considered to belong to a single family stemming from a common ancestor or group of ancestors. On this basis, linguists—the scientists who study language and its origins—have divided the languages of the world into about twenty-five groups.

One of these groups, found to contain about 130 languages spoken by more than half of the people in the world today, is the Indo-European group to which English belongs. How did the linguists come to this conclusion? What do these languages have in common?

Do you want to try your hand at being a language detective? Start with a simple, open-and-shut case: You have five dictionaries in which you can look up the translation for any English word. Four of them are dictionaries of living languages—Italian, Spanish, Portuguese, and French. The fifth is a dictionary of Latin as it was written two thousand years ago. Look up a few words and make a table of them to compare the translations. Your list might look like this:

English	Latin	Italian	Spanish	Portuguese	French
ten	decem	dieci	diez	dez	dix
fire	foco	fuoco	fuego	fogo	feu
gold	auro	oro	oro	ouro	or
horse	caballo	cavallo	caballo	cavalo	cheval
egg	ovo	uovo	huevo	ôvo	oeuf
know	sapere	sapere	saber	saber	savoir

It's not very hard to discover that, on the evidence so far collected, Italian, Spanish, Portuguese, and French all belong to the same family and that their parent language is Latin. From these examples it seems equally clear that English is not a member of this family, because only one word —*fire*—even begins with the same letter. But wait a minute! You're a better detective than that. Can you think of some other words in English that have some connection in meaning with *ten* and *fire* and *gold,* with *horse* and *egg* and *know,* and that sound anything like the ones you have listed? Something about ten? The *deci*mal system? Fire? Nothing comes to mind, and the dictionary is no help because the only words beginning *foc-* have to do with focus, and neither focus nor fog has anything to do with fire. But don't stop there. Gold? There's no familiar word, but try the dictionary again. There it is: *aurous.* It means "containing gold." Horses are in the *cavalry,* of course! And an egg is *oval.* And if *know* stumps you, try the dictionary again. You'll find *sapient,* which means "wise." Here is your new table:

English	Latin
decimal	decem
———	foco
aurous	auro
cavalry	caballo
oval	ovo
sapient	sapere

So for each of the words in your original collection, except for one word: *fire*—the only one that seemed to have a possible connection because it began with the same letter

—you have found a related word. It's time for a new conclusion: English is part of the Latin family, but it has a mixed parentage.

You'd have to be a much more experienced language detective to know where to look next for the other side of the family of English. You need a new set of dictionaries this time: Swedish, German, and Dutch. You might be encouraged, at the start, to find that *feuer* (pronounced foy–er) is the German word for fire. Looking up the words for mother and father you would find.

English	Swedish	German	Dutch
mother	moder	mutter	moeder
father	fader	vater	vader

Clearly there is a close relationship, especially when you learn that the German *v* is pronounced *f,* the *a* is pronounced *ah.* If you know some people who talk about their *fahders* instead of *fathers,* you will realize how close the *th* sound is to *d.*

Just as Latin was found to be the parent of the first group of languages, so this group too has a parent language, which has been given the name of Primitive Germanic. The language is now lost but it is believed to have been spoken about two thousand years ago.

In this way the parentage of English words can be traced back two thousand years in two different families, in much the way that you could go back—though hardly for two thousand years—to find your ancestors on your father's side and on your mother's side.

But wait a minute! Is there a relationship between these two groups, the Latin and the Primitive Germanic? What is there for mother and father in the first group of dictionaries?

Latin	Italian	Spanish	Portuguese	French
mater	madre	madre	mãe	mère
pater	padre	padre	pai	père

The relationship is not so close, but there certainly is a trace of family resemblance. Was there then a common ancestor?

This is how linguists begin to work to group languages by common ancestry. Similar words are the first step. Then it is necessary to notice how the vowels and consonants change from the parent language and to check whether this pattern is followed in other words. If *pater* in Latin becomes *père* in French, and if the Latin word for brother is *frater*, what should you expect the French word for brother to be? How right you are: *frère*! In comparing the Latin and Germanic-group words for father you can see that where the Latin has a *p* the Germanic group has the *f* sound (written *f* or *v*). This pattern does follow through in other words. (Compare the Latin *planus* and the Greek *platus* with the English *flat*; all mean the same.) Brother in Sanskrit was *bhrater*. In Latin it was *frater*. In Greek *phrater*. In German it is *bruder*, in Italian *fratello*. What a fine collection of clues to show how vowels and consonants change!

By means of comparisons of this kind, linguists were able to discover that Indo-European was the grandparent language for almost all the languages of Europe and of some of the Middle East and of Asia as far east as India. No one speaks Indo-European today (nor has, in historic times) and there are no records of the language itself, but linguists make educated guesses about what some of the words or at least the roots may have been. (A root is a part of a word that a whole group of related words have in common. For instance, in English, *pend* is the root of *depend, suspend, appendix*.) The Indo-European root for father was probably *pat,* and for mother, *mat.*

The earliest recorded language of the Indo-European family is Sanskrit. At first it was thought that Indo-European was spoken in India because Sanskrit is the classical language of India as Latin is the classical language of Italy. But, although Sanskrit is a very old language, there is proof that Indo-European is older still. Linguists can reconstruct it from bits of evidence in much the way that archaeologists can reconstruct an ancient city from the fragments of roads and ruins, of pottery and other artifacts that they unearth.

But even if the linguists can reconstruct a lost language from such bits and pieces, how can they tell where and when the language was spoken?

Some of the clues come from facts known outside of the words of the language. It is reasonable to look for the origin of Indo-European languages somewhere in Europe or

Asia because this is where the family languages are spoken today and have been throughout historic times. None of the family is found in the western hemisphere until after Columbus, nor in Africa, Australia, or the Pacific Islands or the Southeast Asia mainland until much later periods when trade and exploration spread languages all over the world. So Indo-European was spoken somewhere in Europe or Asia. Can the territory be narrowed down?

If the only words that a language family had in common were words like *father, mother,* and *brother,* no useful conclusions could be drawn. Wherever and whenever men lived, they had mothers, fathers, and brothers. But there are words as similar in all of the languages of the family that do provide some excellent clues for the language detective.

Do you want to try your hand at detection again? Here are the clues:

These words existed in the Indo-European language, as proved by the resemblance of words in the family of languages:

snow	frost	spring	summer	autumn	winter		
wolf	bear	dog	cow	sheep	goat	pig	horse
plow	spade	sickle	sowing	mowing	mill		
beech tree	gold	copper					

On the other hand, there is no common word in the family and therefore, probably, no Indo-European word for these:

sea	bronze	tin

From the evidence, can you answer these questions?

Did the Indo-Europeans live in a climate of changing temperatures?
Were the winters cold?
Were they farmers?
Had they domesticated any animals?
Did they live inland or on the seacoast?

For two harder questions you need two more items of information, and here they are: (1) Beech trees today are not found growing in the Middle East or in Asia, but they are found in all of Europe as far east as Poland and the Ukraine. (2) Copper was the first metal in the world to be used, beginning about six thousand years ago. When it was discovered that tin could be alloyed with copper to produce bronze, stone tools were abandoned in favor of tools made of cast bronze. In Europe and Asia this discovery was made about thirty-five hundred to four thousand years ago and marks the true end of the Stone Age and the beginning of the Bronze Age.

The questions you're now prepared to guess about are:

When was Indo-European spoken?
Where was it spoken?

There are no certain answers to these questions but, on the evidence, north-central Germany, Lithuania, the Danube Valley, and Ukraine have all been suggested. Tribes coming into Asia Minor from the plains of Asia about four thousand years ago probably were the cause of the breakup of the Indo-Europeans, who then left their homeland and migrated in different directions. They settled in Greece and in Italy, in Persia, in Afghanistan, and in India. They made their way northward to Russia and westward through Central Europe to reach France, Spain, and the British Isles. Perhaps they did not reach the area of Finland and Estonia. Perhaps they skirted Hungary. It might be, because the languages of these areas are the only major European languages that are not related to Indo-European. Perhaps they passed through these territories but did not succeed in imposing their language upon the people who were already there and already speaking a well-developed language. We do not know.

It is not likely that much of the territory they covered in their migrations was wholly unoccupied. It is known, for example, that they crossed the Ionian Sea to the island of Crete, where they overthrew the Minoan civilization, which was already highly advanced, far beyond the culture of the invaders. What languages were spoken in territories they crossed and settled in we do not know because, with one interesting exception, these territories adopted the Indo-European language in one of its many forms. The exception was the Basque language spoken by people who inhabited and still inhabit the border between France and Spain. There are about three-quarters of a million Basque-speaking people today. So far, no connection has been found between Basque and any other language in the world. Perhaps it is the closest we shall come to language spoken by the early people of Europe.

Meanwhile, in other parts of the world, other languages were developing. The earliest of which we have records are the Indo-Chinese group (including Chinese, Thai, Tibetan, and Burmese) first recorded about thirty-five hundred years ago and the Hamito-Semitic group, spoken in northern Africa and in Asia from the Mediterranean to Iran. Of this latter group, Egyptian is the earliest recorded language. Records in pictograph form date back over five thousand years. Among the modern languages of this group, Arabic and Hebrew are the best known.

Other important language groups of this period are the Japanese, the Ural-Altaic (which was perhaps the language of the Asian invaders who dispersed the Indo-Europeans and from which such geographically widely separated languages as Turkish and Finnish developed), the Sudano-Guinean languages of central and southern Africa, the Malayo-Polynesian group of the Pacific Islands, the Papuan group of New Guinea, the native languages of the interior of Australia, and the many different language groups of the Indians of North and South America—now numbering more than one thousand.

How do the linguists know that these languages were not part of the Indo-European family? The same detective system will work in reverse. Try it out with a language of the Hamito-Semitic group. Choose family names like *mother, father,* and *brother* and some other basic words that every language must have a name for, regardless of the time and place when it is spoken. Take, for example, such words as *name, eat, fruit,* and *water* and compare two basic groups of Indo-European, the Latin and the Germanic, with Hebrew, the old Semitic language in which the Old Testament of the Bible was written. Here is a new table:

English	Latin	Germanic	Hebrew
mother	mater	mutter / moder	imma
father	pater	vater / fader	av
brother	frater	bruder / broder	akh*
fruit	fructus	frucht	pree
name	nomen	name (pronounced nah-muh)	shame

Were the Indo-European and the Hamito-Semitic groups once connected, themselves descended from some older parent? Linguists think it is possible but not proven, though here and there one can find some similarities in basic words. For instance the Indo-European word for water was probably *wed* and the descendants of this word—the Latin *aqua* and the Germanic *wazzar*—are not as similar as the Arabic *oued,* "a river," and the Egyptian *hua,* "water." There is some slight similarity, too, between the words for mother and father. A connection might someday be found, since the structure of the Semitic language is like that of the Indo-European at least to the extent that a noun in one language translates into a noun in another and words can be joined into sentences in somewhat similar ways.

This is not true of all languages. Many American Indian languages, for example, do not have sentences made up of

* *kh* shows a gargle sound such as you make clearing your throat, the sound of *ch* in *Bach.*

separate words, as English does. A given syllable has a meaning that changes and works its way up to full sentence meaning by the addition of prefixes and suffixes. The resulting sentence is one word. To say "He invites people to a feast" in the Nootka Indian language, you would start with the syllable for "cooking," add a sound to mean "result," and get, so far, "cooked food." To this you would add "eat" and a syllable meaning "those who" and get, by now, "cooked-food eaters." Then you add on a syllable that means "going for," or "invite," and finally a syllable for "he does." The result is a word, one word, only fifteen letters long. It would obviously be a far more difficult task to show a relationship between the Nootka language and any Indo-European language.

Most linguists doubt that there is any relationship, believing that it is unlikely to be proved that there was originally just one language from which all languages developed. So far, languages have been assembled into about twenty-five groups. But in many cases these groupings are highly inaccurate, being based on geography more than on similarity of words and sentences. The three hundred and fifty North American Indian languages, for example, are sometimes grouped into as few as three groups, according to the areas where they are spoken, but based on similarity of words and structure there are at least twenty-five groups. The largest of these, the Algonquian, has six divisions within it, and a total of fifty-one separate languages.

Are you beginning to have the feeling that nothing is very definite in the science of linguistics? That there are more questions than answers? Nobody is willing to tell you exactly how many languages there are or have been, nor when nor where language originated, nor how many original languages there once were. Can the linguists at least tell you how many words there are in the language you speak? No, not even that.

If you think this is all very unscientific, here's a scientific job for you: Please analyze the Mississippi River, telling how many drops of water there are in it and describing each drop in terms of its position in the river and its relationship to the drops around it.

You can't do it? For shame, Mr. Scientist—why can't you? For the same reason, I suspect, that the linguists cannot tell how many words there are in a language. The language is forever changing, as new words are added, as old words take on new meanings or are lost. Besides, just exactly what is a drop of water? Just exactly what is a word? Do you count words by their spelling or by their meaning? How many words is *run*?

CHAPTER IV

Here Today
and Gone Tomorrow

You have seen how the linguists trace the origin of many present-day languages and known dead languages back to Indo-European. If you agree with their findings, you know that somewhere around 2500 B.C. a group of people who lived perhaps in Central Europe, perhaps in the Middle East, were forced by invaders from Asia to break up and leave their homeland to migrate in many directions and set up new settlements or invade existing settlements. Why did the language change into so many different languages and change so greatly that by the time the Greeks fought the Persians in the sixth century B.C., they had no idea that their languages had a common parent?

For one thing, they all left a common homeland for new territory. They all, therefore, had new experiences in meeting different climates, geography, people. New words would have to be invented to name and describe what they encountered. Even if the new experiences were the same for all groups, there is no reason to suppose all would invent the same new words to represent them. But, of course, the experiences were very different. The people who migrated to the islands of the Aegean Sea and later became Greeks led a very different life from those who went east through Persia to Pakistan and India or north to Germany, Russia, and the Scandinavian peninsula.

But why, you might ask, should the words that were already in their language change? Why should the Indo-European root for mother—*mat*—become *mater* and *madre* and *moder* and *mutter* and *mother*? There is no real answer to the why, but it is easy to see that the same sort of change always does take place, even down to the present day.

Everybody who writes English writes *going to do* but in some parts of America this is pronounced "gonna do" and in others "gwine to do." If there were no written language to tie spoken words together, they would end up as separate words. Then, when the spoken words were eventually reduced to writing, you would find no clearer relation between *gonna* and *gwine to* than you do between *moder* and *mother*.

A person who does pronounce *going to* as "gonna" and has never heard it pronounced in any other way is probably quite confused when he discovers that it's spelled *going to*. He no more understands the spelling of *going to* than you understand the spelling of *light*. He has never heard anyone say *going to,* as you have never heard anyone say *likht*. (That's the same *kh* sound discussed earlier as the sound of *ch* in Bach.) But *likht* is how *light* is pronounced by some Scotsmen today. It is a Germanic word matched exactly by the word for light in modern German: *licht.*

Still, why *gh,* since there's no sound at all of a *g?* The trouble came about because English was written down in the Latin alphabet and English had many sounds for which there were no letters in the Latin alphabet. For some of these sounds new letters were invented: *j,* for example. For others, combinations of letters were used: *th, sh, ch.* First *h* alone and later *gh* was used for the sound of *kh.*

When the pronunciation of *light* changed, the spelling remained the same, just as *going to* will remain in spite of all the people who pronounce it "gonna."

Some of the peculiarities of English spelling occurred because English took over words from other languages along with the spelling of the original language, but people then pronounced the words in ways that fitted in well with English pronunciation. Words beginning with *ch-* and taken from the Greek—words like *chaos, chorus,* and *Christian* —changed the *kh* sound of the Greek to a simple *k* sound. Those that were taken from the French—like *chain* and *chief*—changed the *sh* sound of the French. Words more recently taken from French—like *chivalry* and *chef*—keep the French pronunciation.

Some modern examples of what happens to the spelling and pronunciation of borrowed words may make this process easier to understand. The *zz* in *pizza* is obviously not the *zz* in *fizzle.* We spell and pronounce *pizza* as the Italians do. But when we took over from the French the name for a chair-becoming-a-sofa, a "long chair," as the French call it: *chaise longue,* many people thought of it as a lounge, so that the spelling and pronunciation *chaise lounge* are now quite common and are even to be found in the dictionary. Simpler examples are the names of foreign cities. We spell Paris and Berlin as the French and Germans do, but we do not pronounce them as they do. In France, Paris is *pah-ree'* and in Germany, Berlin is *bare-leen'*. We have changed both the spelling and pronunciation of Brazil. The Brazilians spell it Brasil and pronounce it with an *s*, not a *z*.

More interesting, perhaps, than changes in spelling and pronunciation are changes in the meaning of words. Even in such well-developed and formal languages as present-day English, any number of local dialects arise. Not only pronunciation but word usage changes from one country to another and from one part of a country to another part. You ride elevators in America, but lifts in England. Here you watch TV; in England it's the telly. In New York and Connecticut, bags are made of paper and sacks are made of rough cloth. Exactly the opposite is true in Missouri.

In making a study of dialects in rural England, investigators went to over three hundred localities of which none was more than fifteen miles away from the next. In their travels they found eighty-eight different ways of saying "left-handed." Some samples: back-handed, buck-fisted, coochy-gammy, cow-pawed, gammy-palmed, gibble-fisted, keggy, left-cooched, north-handed, skiffy, squiffy, and watted.

The object of such research is to prepare a linguistic atlas, a collection of maps showing what word meanings and what pronunciations are found in particular regions and discovering to what extent they overlap. Such atlases exist for countries all over the world.

Words often take on special local meanings. A teacher in a new one-story school was baffled when one of her pupils asked permission to go to the basement. She was quite sure there was no basement. There wasn't, but there had been in the school from which her pupils had been transferred and that was where the washrooms were. They had been asking permission to go to the basement for years. The phrase had a new and permanent meaning for them.

This is an example of a private meaning among a very small group of people, but there are many instances in English where words acquire new meanings in special circumstances and these meanings stick and may even outlast the first meanings. An *arbitrary* decision: what does that mean? It could mean simply that it is a decision made by an *arbiter* or *arbitrator* (a kind of judge appointed to settle a dispute and make an award). That was its original meaning, and the word is still so used. But it's much more likely to mean that it is a decision made without good reason, at the whim of the person who made it. There must have been quite a few arbiters' decisions that people considered to be unfair for this meaning to have taken hold.

Some words have come so far from their first meanings that it would be hard for you to guess what those early meanings were. *Manufacture* is straight from the Latin: "to make by hand." *Dexterous* and *sinister* are two more good examples. These words come directly from Latin, where they meant "right-handed" and "left-handed." But then *right* comes to mean correct and proper and is used in such terms as *right-hand man*. *Dexterous* then becomes skillful, whether with the right hand or the left. Meanwhile, *left* becomes a term of disapproval, as a *left-handed* compliment, and someone who is clumsy is said to have two *left* feet. Along with this, *sinister* develops much nastier meanings: wrong, dishonest, disastrous, and evil. French follows the same pattern: *droit,* which means right (hand), has all the other meanings of English *right* and, in addition, means *law*. *A droit*—"on the right"—becomes "skillful," in French and later in English, as one word, *adroit*. *Gauche* —the left hand—means awkward, clumsy, and crooked and has been taken over into English with these meanings, where it has gone even further, to mean tactless and lacking in social graces.

Correct English used to be called the King's English. Indeed it was. Consider all the favorable words you can use in describing someone, and look at their sources. *Chivalrous* (from *chevalier*—"a knight," formerly simply "a horseman"); *courteous* ("having court manners"); *generous* and *gentle, gentlemen* and *gentlewomen* (from the Latin *gentilis* —"of the same clan"—and then meaning "well-born"); *noble* ("of the nobility"). Now look at the unfavorable words: *ignoble* (the opposite of *noble*); *villain* (from the Latin *villa,* "a farm," and hence "a peasant"); *vulgar* (Latin for "of the common people"); *boor* (from the Germanic *boer,* "a farmer"). The hick or country bumpkin is a stupid lout, while the *urbane* man ("the man of the city") is sophisticated, polished, courteous.

Words of this kind, whose original meaning has been wholly lost, present no problem to today's readers of English. Nobody, asked what he does for a living, is going to say he's a "boor" or a "villain." The confusion comes when old sayings and proverbs survive in the language although the meaning of the words in them has been lost. The early meanings can still be found in the dictionary, marked *arch.* (archaic) or *obs.* (obsolete), but the trouble is that no one looks for the words in the dictionary because they are common words whose meaning people think they know.

What does the proverb "The exception proves the rule" mean to you? Some people think it means that if there is an exception to a rule, that proves the rule is a good one, though why that should be, it's hard to imagine. But *proves,* in this case, does not mean "furnishes evidence." Nor does it necessarily mean that in the sentence "You can prove your strength by lifting this heavy weight." In these contexts, *prove* means "test." You can test the rule by finding whether it has any exceptions. That was the original meaning of *prove,* from the Latin *probare,* to test. Perhaps the tests were often satisfactory so that *prove* came to mean "make a satisfactory test" and hence "demonstrate the validity of something" as now, in proving an accusation of guilt at a trial or in proving your point.

Prove is an interesting word because it seems to have come full circle in its meanings. *Prove* and *proof* come from the Latin *probus,* which means good, honest, and proper. From that comes *probare,* the verb, which means "to find or think good." From that comes *proba,* "a test." All these meanings coexist in English in one form or another. To *probe* is to search out and test. *Probity* is honesty and goodness. To *prove* is to conduct a successful test. And words like *approve* and *improve* show their relationship. Some others are trickier. How you get from *proba* to the meaning of *reprobate* and *reproof* ("a scoundrel" and "a scolding") is quite mysterious, since the prefix *re-* means only "again." No explanation is offered by the dictionaries. Was there perhaps a confusion between the syllables *repro-* and the prefix *retro-*, which means "backward"?

Another word like *prove* whose meaning everyone knows is *try*. You wouldn't look it up in the dictionary. But then you come upon a direction in an old cookbook: "Try the fat in a spider." What in heaven's name are you supposed to do? Take a chunk of solid fat, put it in a skillet on a hot stove, and wait till the fat melts. To *try* fat is to *render* it. And this might not help you either if you know *render* in terms of *rendering* aid or *rendering* a German poem into English. *Trying* fat in a spider may well *try* your patience. And what does *try* mean here? We're back to *prove*.

What does the proverb "Waste not, want not" mean to you? The tricky word is *want,* and it appears with the same meaning in "Man wants but little here below." It's not that saving string and potato peelings will so enrich you that you will have no *desire* for anything else. But you will not *want*—you will not *be in need,* or be poverty-stricken. This is also the meaning of *want* that makes sense of the psalm, "The Lord is my shepherd. I shall not want."

A rather curious example of how the current meaning of

a word is mistakenly applied to older writing occurs in the King James version of the Bible, which was translated from the Latin. In Psalm 119, there is the line: "I prevented the dawning of the morning." How could one do that? The word *prevent* stems from the Latin *prae-*, "before," and *ventum,* a part of the verb "to go." The Jewish Bible, which is translated directly from the Hebrew and did not come through the Latin translation, has for this verse: "I rose early at dawn."

These days you can watch words change before your eyes. (Really, you're hearing them change before your ears, but that doesn't sound quite right, does it?) For example, if you listened to the commentators and the conversation between the astronauts of the *Apollo 15* space flight and Mission Control, you picked up a whole bunch of new usages for old words. When the third parachute failed to open on the descent of the capsule, it wasn't serious because only two parachutes were really necessary for a safe landing and the third was therefore redundant. If you look up *redundant* in the dictionary you will find that this usage does match the dictionary definition—"superfluous, more than necessary." But before 1971, the word had most often been used in reference to superfluous words, information, and the like. The synonym the dictionary gives is *wordy.*

You will not find in the dictionary the meaning given by the astronauts to the word *anomaly.* They used it to mean any malfunction (poor performance) of any instrument. The closest the dictionary comes to this is *irregularity,* but in general the word has meant an object or situation out of keeping with the normal or expected. The cart before the horse, for example, is a classic anomaly.

All through the conversation, instead of saying, "We understand," Mission Control said, "We copy."

But perhaps the neatest change in meaning is what happened to the word *geology*. Derived from the Greek words *geo*—"earth"—and *-logy*—"study of," *geology* until then had meant "the study of the earth's crust, especially as recorded in rocks." How can a geological expedition to the moon study earth's rocks? A new word—*lunology*—is needed, but it hasn't been coined yet.

The word *deploy*, originally only a military term meaning "to spread out in battle formation," now seems to mean "to put into operation." The lunar rover—of which, after all, there was just one—was *deployed*, hardly in battle formation.

During this space flight, *eyeball* was firmly established as a verb meaning to look at something directly, rather than through the lens of some optical instrument.

Words come and go. The slang of one period may be entirely unintelligible at a later date. Do you understand any of these?

She gave me the glad eye.
That dress makes her look as if she's just off the boat.
He acts like a greenhorn.
Shake a leg.
I'm fit to be tied.
She's no chicken.
Tell it to the marines.

(43)

As for the slang of the last decade, here is one comment:

SONG OF THE SQUARES

We're well over thirty, we're obsolete men
And we'll have to learn English all over again.
LIKE MAN, to our thinking's an ape of some kind.
If you said, "OUT OF SIGHT," we'd think, "Out
   of mind."
ROCK AND ROLL means the baby RIGHT ON the
   tree top
In a comfortable cradle. The *weasel* goes POP.
Only toddlers in tantrums are MAKING THE SCENE
And NO SWEAT is a sign that you keep yourself clean.
If a man's OUT TO LUNCH, he's eating at noon
And if he's FAR OUT, don't phone back too soon.
The people who SPLIT are like Jekyll and Hyde
Taken off to a hospital, locked up inside.
The only connection between GRASS and HORSE
Is that Dobbin might feed on the green stuff, of course.
BREAD should be buttered, a PAD is to write on.
We never TURN ON; we just turn the light on.
DIG YOU? We wouldn't unless you had died.
BLOW OUR MINDS? Why that's nothing but plain
   suicide.
Your words sound familiar; your meaning is not.
We don't know what's cooking. We've just gone to pot.
We're well over thirty, we're obsolete men
And we'll have to learn English all over again.

Some slang words, though, will find a permanent place in the language. *Neat* will probably do so, as *nice* did a long time back. People who are fond of English for its wide variety of close but not exactly equivalent synonyms, for its subtle shades of meaning, and for its precision are disturbed when its nice distinctions are blurred. (Do you know the meaning of *nice* in that sentence? It doesn't mean "pleasant and agreeable.") They feel that it is better to have such a variety of words as *like, love, want, desire,* and *need,* than, like Spanish, to have one word that means all of these. People who say "I love pancakes" are losing the advantage of English. So, too, when we create hundreds of equivalents for *very. Very* is good enough. It serves. Why make *awfully* and *terribly* (which were once wonderful words) into nothing but synonyms for *very?* What kind of contradiction is involved in saying that a conversation is awfully silly or terribly kind? (That's terrific! Is it terrible and tremendously good all at once?) Hollywood and Madison Avenue have stripped of all meaning such once-splendid words as *superb, colossal, magnificent.*

But language is a group product and, because it is, it will grow and change as the community that uses it grows and changes, like it or not. The rules of a language, the meanings of the words in it, are not something decided in advance like the rules of a game. Dictionaries and grammar textbooks serve only to record and explain what the language means to the people who use it, so that people new to the group—either children or foreigners—can find out how best to make themselves understood.

These days, television has a far greater influence on the English language than a dictionary or grammar or teacher of English can have. It will doubtless have the effect of bringing dialects together again and eliminating many of the differences in speech patterns in the United States, simply because the same word meanings, pronunciations, and usages enter the homes of people all over the country and tend to standardize the language.

An army of English teachers can no longer stem the tide of *like* used as a conjunction. The constant repetition of the cigarette commercial—originally intended as an attention-getter to draw the groans of grammarians—has had an irreversible effect. Though the commercial is long gone, "like it should" is part of the language now.

English teachers will also have to surrender to *lay* as a synonym for *lie*. Too many television speakers don't know the difference, and the teachers (some of whom don't know the difference themselves) are hopelessly outnumbered. Whether this is a good thing or not is really beside the point.

CHAPTER V

Word Building— from Aback to Zany

So far we've been talking about how the basic words in languages change in spelling, pronunciation, and meaning over the years. But how about the normal way of making new words and combining them? A language must have some rules for doing this if people are to understand each other's new words. All languages do, but the rules vary from one language to another within a family group and vary even more widely from one family group to another.

In all Indo-European languages, there are root words to which prefixes and suffixes can be added to change such aspects of the word as the time of action of a verb (its tense —present, past, or future), from the action of a verb to a noun—the person or thing acting or acted upon, the number involved, and other such. For example, from the root word *act* we can make *acting* and *acted*. For the future tense English needs a helping verb: *will act*, but many other Indo-European languages, of which Latin is the strictest of all, add a suffix for future tense just as English does for the past tense. From *act* we can also make *action* and *actor, active* and *activate*. Starting at the other end, we can add a prefix to get *react, inactive*. We can do this with noun roots as well: from the root word *friend,* we make *friendly, befriend, friendship,* and *friendless.* Starting with an adjective such as *sterile* or *civic* we can make *sterilize* and *civilize.* With an adjective such as *sweet* or *hard,* we can make *sweeten* and *harden.* We can add *-s* (or *-es*) to most words to show plural (more than one) and *-'s* to show a relation of possession. We can also use back-formations, making *beg* from *beggar, sculpt* from *sculptor, edit* from *editor.*

If you know the meaning of prefixes and suffixes, you can make up new words as needed and people will understand you. *Oneupmanship* and *gamesmanship* are made-up words whose meanings are clear. You don't need to consult a dictionary for such very recent words as *trivialize* and *weightlessness.*

Languages of other family groups do not necessarily operate by adding prefixes and suffixes to root words in this way. In the Semitic languages, Arabic and Hebrew, for example, the root word consists of consonants only, and the meaning is changed by changing the vowel sounds between the consonants. English has some words that do this: for example, *sing.* We change *sing* not to *singed* but to *sang* and *sung* for changes in time, and to *song* for a change from verb to noun.

Written Hebrew and Arabic is somewhat like Speedwriting, because only the essential elements of the word are written down. In these languages, only the consonants appear.

Cn y rd ths sntnc prfctl wll wtht vwls?

Fairly well. The words taken separately would cause trouble, because *rd* could be *rod* or *rid* or *ride* or *road* or *rode* or *red,* but in context, it can't possibly be anything else but *read.* The Semitic-language reader is helped by the fact that most root words consist of exactly three consonants with vowels between them, as in English words like *rebel, favor, cover.* The consonants are never doubled, nor are two different consonants joined in a single syllable. Besides, if a word begins with a vowel or contains two vowels not separated by a consonant (as in *piano*), a special silent consonant would be used to show this. Thus *dd* could stand for *did, dad, dead, dud,* but could not possibly be *eddie* or *added.*

If *rebel* were a Hebrew noun, you would change it to *robel,* perhaps, to mean "one who rebels," to *rabil* to mean "a rebellion," to *robol* to mean "he rebelled," and so on. Indo-European languages do this occasionally—there are the irregular verbs like *sing* and *drink*—where the Semitic languages use it as the regular method. But Semitic languages also use prefixes and suffixes for other changes in word meaning.

Thus *s-f-r* is the root word for "tell," *safor* is "to write," *sufor* is "to be told or declared," *safer* is "a book," *saf'rut* is "literature," and *sif'reah* is "a library."

(49)

Some other languages make no distinction at all between verbs and nouns. In Malay, for example, there are no parts of speech as such. A word can be used for anything. A single word could mean either *my food* or *eat me*. In a very limited way, English is like this: *hard* is both an adjective and an adverb. When you do hard work, you work hard, though the usual rule is: when you do neat work, you work neatly. *Lecture* is both a noun and a verb. When you lecture, you give a lecture. The usual form is: when you paint, you make a painting.

Besides the rules for adding prefixes and suffixes, there are usually rules for making compound words. These rules vary a great deal from one language to another. German, for example, regularly makes words by stringing together almost any number of separate words to form a new compound word. You could have a single word like *Fordautomobilepartassemblybusinesscorporation*. In English you are not so free to do this and often, when you do put words together to form a new word, the new word means something different from its separate parts. *Roadblock* and *bedroom* are examples of the usual kind. *Touchdown* and *comedown* are examples of the second type. In Chinese, many compounds are made whose meaning can be understood only by adding the meaning of the two parts and averaging them. Thus *light-heavy* means "weight," *much-little* means "size," *survival-destruction* means "existence." You must also be very careful in English about the order in which you put words together. Outlay and layout, uphold and holdup, upset and setup, outlook and lookout, farewell and welfare are typical of the problems you face.

Knowing which suffix to add is important. *Contentness* and *happiment* won't work. It's also necessary to be able to recognize a suffix when you see one. Sometimes people pick up word endings and attach these endings to other words in the belief that they are adding a suffix. *Hamburger* becomes *cheeseburger,* as if a hamburger were a burger made of ham, instead of a food named after the city of Hamburg. The Automat was so named because it was a self-service restaurant that delivered food automatically when coins were deposited. Thereafter, words like *laundromat* were coined. But if a laundromat deals with laundry then an automat would have to deal with autos, not foods. What's a *twinight* ball game? Logically it should be one played on two nights, because twilight is so named because of the two kinds of light.

But let's suppose you are not fooled by fake suffixes; you know all the rules and are prepared to follow them. How well do the rules work in English?

Start with the simplest of rules: add the suffix -*ed* to change a verb from the present tense to the past tense: Today I *walk;* yesterday I *walked.* Today I *run* and yesterday I *runed.* Today I *bring* and yesterday I *bringed.* There seems to be some problem here.

A pleasant two-player game can be built around this problem. Take two words whose endings in the present tense are spelled the same way—like *sing* and *wing*—and interchange their past tenses. See whether your opponent can unscramble them. Here are a whole bunch of pairs like this to play with:

The bird *singed* as he *wang* his way over the hills.

The professor *teached* them all day long, but he did not feel that he had *raught* the class or that they understood the work.

I had *sleeped* for only five hours when the car horn *bept* me awake.

When I woke the boy to give him his medicine, he *blank* his eyes in the bright light and cried, but he *drinked* his medicine.

It was a terrible blizzard, and the wind *blowed* hard all night as it *snew* and *snew*.

They *fighted* a good fight and *rought* all the wrongs that had been done.

When we *swimmed* in the pool, we asked the owner to make the pool lights brighter, but instead he *dam* them.

After I *winned* the contest, the principal *pon* a medal on me.

My friend never *speaked* to me again after I *snoke* into his tree house without permission.

Joe ran away when he was accused of a crime he didn't commit. My father said he shouldn't have run, but I *sid* with Joe and said I would have *hided* him and helped him to escape.

These examples are fairly easy to solve because one of the pair of words does follow the rule and adds -*ed* to make the past tense. But if neither one of the pair has a regular past tense, the puzzles are more difficult to solve: This one's medium hard.

I *get* the shelf up on the wall before the glue *sot*. (*Set-set* and *get-got* leads to *set-sot* and *get-get*.)
I *writ* my mother a letter telling how the dog *bote* me. (*Bite-bit* and *write-wrote* leads to *bite-bote* and *write-writ*.)

Now it gets harder:

I *maid* have been able to reach him by phone, but I don't know what I would have *sight* if I had. (May and say.)

And here's a really tough one:

I *gid* and *zent* what I had to do.

And if you're going to solve that one, you had better go and do it.

Try some other suffixes. From a group of words like *childless, hopeless, penniless,* and *tasteless,* it's easy to see that -*less* is a genuine suffix and that it means "without." The suffix works even in some words where it seems not to at first glance—words like *listless* and *hapless*. Without *list?* Yes, because there was such a word in Middle English (now long lost) and it meant "desire." *Hap,* also a Middle English word, derived from Old Norse, meant "good luck." Does *fruitless* mean without *fruit?* Yes, in its basic meaning it does. A fruitless plan doesn't bear fruit; it yields nothing.

-Less seems to be a useful suffix, especially since new words can be made whenever needed—*topless* bathing suits, for example. Yes, but . . . how about *helpless* and *restless?*

How about *selfless?* In a sense, yes—a selfless action is not one without self, but it is one without thought of self. Accept it. But the opposite of *selfless* is *selfish.* So the opposite of *hopeless* should be *hopish* and of *childless, childish!*

Another useful suffix is *-en.* Add it to an adjective to form a verb. From such words as *quicken, thicken, sweeten, sicken,* it's obvious that *-en* means to make. Yes, obvious. So if the food that I ate *sickened* me, I'll go to the doctor to see if he can *wellen* me.

The suffix *-ly* can be added to adjectives to make adverbs. It can also be added to nouns, in which case *-ly* means like a ————: *brotherly, princely, motherly, manly,* and so on. Too bad that although John Doe, Sr., has a *fatherly* affection for John Doe, Jr., the latter has no *sonly* feelings for his father.

Sometimes when the root-plus-suffix doesn't mean what it ought to, it's your understanding of the root, not the suffix, that's at fault. From words like *awesome* and *fearsome,* you can conclude that the suffix *-some* means "having the quality of or provoking." Something awesome provokes awe. If you happen to know that *win* (or *wyn*) was the Anglo-Saxon word for "joy," then you'll know that a *winsome* person provokes joy and pleasure. What are you going to do with *handsome?* It ought to mean something like "handy." Well, once it did. It meant "skillful and dexterous." But on this basis do you conclude that a *noisome* thing is noisy? In fact, noisome things offend not the ears but the nose. The word is really *annoysome,* but the beginning was lost. This is the kind of change that is quite frequent in language. If you heard someone say "a newt" and had never heard of the small lizard he was referring to, you would not be sure whether to write it "a newt" or "an ewt." In fact, it was originally "an ewt." Later it became a *newt.* Say, "An orange." Then look at the Spanish word for orange—*naranja* —and you can guess what happened.

Do the rules for adding prefixes work about as well? The prefix *in-* means "not," as in *indecent* and *insignificant.* So *infamous* ought to mean "not famous." How does it come to mean "wicked"?

A delightful game was invented by Marian Forer, as a contributor to the "Trade Winds" column of the *Saturday Review.** She noted that lawyers are disbarred and priests are unfrocked when they are dismissed from their professions. She wondered what happens when other jobs are lost. She suggested that electricians get delighted, musicians get denoted, cowboys are deranged, dressmakers are unbiased, models are deposed, and office workers are defiled.

If you play this game as I have, you'll find that far worse fates await certain professionals. There was the unfortunate Major League player who was debased and the club president who was dismembered! When the accountant was disfigured, the missionary was distracted.

* November 28, 1964. © 1964 Saturday Review, Inc.

For some, the situation was embarrassing rather than tragic. The judge who had been found guilty of accepting a bribe was immediately disrobed, and the violinist who was present at the time was disconcerted.

The travel agent came off better than most. He was merely detoured. The acrobat, however, was thoroughly defeated.

Nothing in particular happened to the Miss America beauty queen; she was merely dismissed, but the carpenter became quite unhinged when he heard about it, and the printer, too, was depressed. The seamstress, who never liked Miss America anyway, was quite unruffled, but Miss America's sister, the hairdresser, was distressed, and her father, a furniture dealer, was unconsoled. The banker, however, couldn't have cared less; he was quite disinterested.

What happens to teachers? They're declassed, degraded, and thoroughly detested. In fact, the teacher of calculus was utterly disintegrated, and the chemistry teacher faced dissolution.

If you don't like puns, please close your eyes and skip the next sentence because our questions are, going back to biblical times, Was Cain disabled? Was Adam deceived?

As long as we're on the subject of rules, let's leave word formations for the moment and look at the rules for pronunciation. Probably your second grade teacher tried to convince you that there are some. Short vowels and long ones. "When two vowels walk together, the first one says its name," or some such good advice. Try and tell your rules to the foreigner who, in despair, wrote this verse:

(56)

I never will learn to read English aloud.
There's *mowed, towed* and *rowed,* but then there's *allowed.*
And once I had finally learned to say *move,*
I met *love, shove* and *dove,* and what did it *prove?*
It *proves* that I'll never discover the *coves*
Where the treasure was found, nor the *stoves* nor the
    groves.
What a merciless language, where *thread* rhymes with *bread*
But *plead* goes with *lead* (though the metal is *lead*)!
And *food* rhymes with *brood,* and also with *mood,*
But *stood* rhymes with *good,* and also with *hood,*
While nothing but *mud* rhymes with *flood* and with *blood.*
Cut goes with *cull* and *put* goes with *pull*
And then I come up with a *but* and a *bull.*
The dog has *gone* off and he's *done* with his *bone.*
As for me, can I travel to *town* on my *own?*
I'll *rush* over to *push* the poor child through the door
But I don't think I'll *put* up with this any more.
Wear a *boot* on your *foot,* push the *hoe* with your *shoe*
But wherever you *go,* don't do what I *do.*
You can say that you've *heard* that the prince grew a *beard.*
The *heir* to the throne? That's really quite *weird.*
There's *blew* and there's *blow,* there's *knew* and there's *know*
And as soon as I've learned it, there's *sew* and there's *sow.*
What a language where *manslaughter's* surely a crime
But *man's laughter*—same letters—will give you no rhyme!
"I have *paid* for the *plaid.*" That is just what he *said!*
I'll never *read* English as it should be *read.*

The despairing foreigner will not fare much better with
consonant pairs:

The wi*ng*ed creatures were *sing*ed by the fire.

What a *ch*ore to have to wear my *ch*iffon dress to sing in the school *ch*oir!

Did the bi*sh*op have a mi*sh*ap of some kind?

I was mis*l*ed about the location of the i*sl*e!

Do you *th*ink *th*ere's anything new growing in the hot-*h*ouse?

Has a*ny*one photographed the ca*ny*on?

Have you a *ph*oto of the cho*ph*ouse?

Have fun trying to respell ordinary words by choosing the spelling of the sounds from other words. The most famous of these is *ghoti*, which spells *fish*, if you have the right clues: *gh* as in *laugh*, *o* as in *women*, and *ti* as in *nation*. How about *psolophubt?* The clues are: *ps* as in *psalm*, *olo* as in *colonel*, *ph* as in *phone*, *u* as in *busy*, and *bt* as in *doubt*. But then the real spelling—surfeit—isn't so obvious either. What can you make by rearranging the *u* from *bury*, the *pt* from *ptomaine*, and the *gn* from *sign*?

Have you ever envied the Spanish child for whom spelling is not even a subject in school, since every vowel and consonant in Spanish has an unvarying pronunciation? If that worked in English, if you knew how to spell *knew*, for instance, and *moan*, you would know how to spell *knew-moania*. Don't envy the Spanish boy when he starts to learn English. The only rules there are for English spelling are negative ones. You can't have more than five consonants together (*lengthwise* has five). You usually can't have more than three vowels together. (*Beauty* has three, and so do all

words ending in *-ious*), but *miaoued* has five. You can't
have a *q* without a *u*, except in some names taken directly
from languages such as Arabic. That's about it. A parlor
game very popular about thirty years ago involved guessing
in what English word certain outlandish combinations of
letters occurred in the order given. Can you find answers to
-ghth-, -mpsi-, -nwh-? They're all common words.

Spelling apart, what rules of pronunciation will be followed when the Spanish boy begins to try to read aloud?
I'm sure you won't have any trouble reading this verse.
Every two lines rhyme, in couplets. I suggest you read it
aloud to yourself in practice for what's to come after it:

I had a date but I called it off
Because I had a dreadful *cough*.

I sounded hoarse and mean and gruff,
My voice was gravelly and rough.

And if I kept my date with you
We'd have a fight and we'd be through.

Besides, I'd hate it if you caught
A cold from me, and so I thought

It best to say I wouldn't go.
This way, you'll save a lot of dough.

And then again, it's raining out.
Thank heaven! after that long drought!

So go and find yourself a pickup
While I stay home to sneeze and hiccough.

(59)

But suppose a foreigner were trying to write a verse like that. Suppose he had a good reading knowledge of English and knew the meanings of all the words, but hadn't quite mastered the pronunciation of -*ough*. This is what he might have written. Please read it aloud as he wrote it, remembering that, as before, each two lines rhyme as a couplet.

I cannot keep my date with you
Because I have a dreadful cough.

And since, after that awful drought,
It's raining and I shouldn't get caught,

As I surely would if I went out,
Really it was best, I thought,

To stay at home and call you up
And tell you, you can save your dough.

I really have to call it off
Because my throat is sore and rough.

Please don't think me curt and gruff.
If you're about to say, "We're through,"

I'll cry and scream and maybe hiccough
And if I'm mad enough I'll kick you.

CHAPTER VI

Is That Mother in the Bottle?

Suppose you have written and typed up an article for the school paper and handed it in for publication. The editors intend to print it by a photocopy process, so you have had to make a neat job of typing. The editor hands your paper back to you, points to a line on page 2, and says, "Can you justify that line?" Does he want you to explain to him the basis for your conclusion or does he want you to retype it so that the end of the line meets the margin?

Can you tell from the following conversation alone whether the track meet is under way or not?

"The team from Old Town just phoned in to say they can't get here till four o'clock."
"Oh rats! We can't hold the track meet till then."

Does "can't hold the track meet" mean "can't start the meet" or does it mean "can't *keep* it going that long"? There's no way to tell.

(61)

There are many words like *hold* and *justify* and *arbitrary* that persist in the language with two or more contrasting meanings. Mostly, though, you can tell from the context what is meant. "I'll read it *presently*" means "Stop nagging me. I won't do it right now, but I'll get around to it soon." But "I'm *presently* reading it" means "I'm reading it right now."

To *dispose* materials is to put them to good use, but to *dispose of* them is to get rid of them. You listen hard to get the *drift* of an argument—to find out where it's going; but if the argument *drifts,* it's going nowhere in particular.

Dry is the opposite of *wet*. So what on earth is a *dry* wine? And what's *dry* toast? (Who'd want it soggy?) And what's a *dry* run over a target? *Dry* humor? A *dry* book? So *dry* is not only wet, but having no sugar, having no butter, having no ammunition, having no emotional expression, and just plain dull.

Consider the witch on her lunch hour. Witchery doesn't pay too well these days, so the witch spends her working day in a factory assembling widgets. But her lunch hours are her own and she does what she pleases during them. At lunch today, *the witch made a monster fast while she ate.* You can read this three ways: She let the poor monster go hungry while it watched her eat. She tied it to the factory gate. She created it rather rapidly while she was munching the eye of a newt and the toe of a frog on dry toast. After you have explained this story to a foreigner who's just learning English, you might tell him (if you're unsympathetic to foreigners) that fast colors don't run.

(62)

A computer, programmed with about three thousand grammatical rules and twenty thousand words, was given the task of analyzing English sentences in all the ways allowed by the rules it had been given. For the sentence "Time flies like an arrow" it offered three interpretations:

1. Determine the speed of flies as quickly as you can.
2. Time passes rapidly.
3. A species of fly, called time flies, enjoy an arrow.

A computer expert, commenting on these results, pointed out that if you were programming this computer to translate English, you could probably program it to choose the correct solution, but what would it then do with the sentence "Fruit flies like bananas"? What would the computer do with these two sentences?

1. Don't cough till you're blue in the face.
2. Don't shoot till you see the whites of their eyes.

"Six Suits Thrown Out," reads the headline. Someone is cleaning out his closet? No, the Supreme Court has denied a hearing in six cases.

These ambiguities—confusion due to double meanings —are caused by the changes in meanings of words like *arbitrary* over the years. Other and more confusing situations arise when words from entirely different sources sound the same and sometimes are even spelled the same. Is the new town hall about to be *raised* or is it about to be *razed?*

(63)

No real trouble arises if you happen to know the meaning of both words and must simply choose the meaning that is right for the context. But suppose you know the meaning of only one and do not even suspect that there is another meaning?

What would it mean to you to read in an old English novel that at the end of dinner the hostess suggested to her guests that they "repair to the drawing room"? Would you try the dictionary for *repair*? *Repair* goes back to an old Indo-European root, *per*. It means "to procure, to produce." Therefore *to repair* is "to produce again" and hence "to fix or mend." But the *repair* of the "repair to the drawing room" comes from the Latin *pater*, "father," through such words as *repatriate*—"go back to the fatherland"— and from there to Old French *repairer*—"to go back." And what did they do in the *drawing room*? Draw? No, they just sat and talked. *Drawing room* is a shortened form of *withdrawing room*, the room to which the ladies withdrew while the gentlemen smoked their after-dinner cigars and talked of matters unseemly for female ears.

Sometimes words drop out of the language because they sound too much like other words and create misunderstandings. *Niggardly*, for example, means "stingy." It has no connection with *Negro*, which comes from the Latin *niger*, "black," but the sound of the word will bar it from the language if it has not already done so.

What about the title of this book and this chapter? Is it a joke? Did it occur to you to look up the word *mother* to find out what the question might possibly mean? Of course you know the meaning of *mother,* but is the mother you know likely to be in a bottle? There is some *mother* that can be. How can the word *mother* mean two such different things? Because it has two separate histories. The history of one you already know. It comes from the Indo-European word that was the parent both of the Latin *mater* and of the Germanic *moder.* The mother in the bottle stems from a root that also gave the Middle German *mudde* and the Middle Dutch *modder,* which meant mud, slime, dregs.

What makes words like *mother* and *repair,* like *prove* and *try,* especially difficult is that it doesn't occur to anyone to look them up in the dictionary. Everybody knows their meaning, so if a sentence doesn't quite make sense, it is treated with a shrug of the shoulders, and the reader goes on to the next sentence.

What are the hardest words in the language? Some people think that words like *lexicographer, intravenous, entomologist,* and *pseudonym* are hard words. They aren't really. They may be unfamiliar. You may have to look up their meanings, spelling, and pronunciation in the dictionary, but once you've looked them up it's quite easy to understand what they mean and how to use them. The hard words are the words it doesn't occur to you to look up. If you do look them up, you're often no further ahead than you were before. They are words that have so many meanings that you can't pin them down. The word *run* has over forty different uses, and a *run* on the bank, a *run* in your stocking, a *run* on the ball field, and *run* of the mill have almost nothing in common. Still, once the word is in its context, you can discover which meaning is appropriate. The really hard words are those that context alone does not solve.

Take the word *before*. Any six-year-old will tell you that he knows the meaning of *before*. Then read him the sentence "The prince came and bowed before the king." Ask him, "Did the king bow? If so, who bowed first?" he will tell you, "The prince did, of course. He bowed *before* the king." How might these sentences be written without using the word *before?*

1. *Before* the Spanish exploration, horses were unknown in Latin America.

2. When you come *before* the committee on admissions to college, be sure to wear your neatest and most becoming clothes.

3. *L* comes *before M* in the alphabet.

4. Don't come *before* seven, as we'll still be at dinner.

5. The question of the man's guilt or innocence is now *before* the court.

6. What a splendid career lies *before* you.

7. If you arrive *before* me, please open the windows.

8. The committee is debating all legislation on ecology now *before* Congress.

9. Wasn't that a dainty dish to set *before* the king?

10. He would endure any torture *before* telling the names of those who helped him to escape.

11. I never did this *before*.

12. Do you put pleasure *before* business?

If you write these sentences with the greatest possible accuracy, you will find that not only are you not using the word *before,* you aren't using the same word twice to replace it. (See footnote if you're stuck.)

The words *beside* and *besides* are almost as difficult. Try replacing them in these sentences:

Who is sitting *beside* him?

This car seems junky *beside* a Cadillac.

That's *beside* the point.

I don't know how to play chess: *besides,* I don't want to.

He was *beside* himself with joy.

Did anyone *besides* Harry pass the test?

Do you know a two-letter word that can mean any one of the following:

concerning

containing

made from

belonging to

for

1. in advance of; 2. in the presence of; 3. ahead of; 4. earlier than; 5. under the jurisdiction of; 6. in the future for; 7. sooner than; 8. under consideration by; 9. in front of; 10. rather than; 11. in time past; 12. consider pleasure more important than.

from
about
born in
who is

among many other meanings? The word, of course, is *of*.

A dream	concerning	flying.
A bottle	containing	soda.
Cloth	made from	gold.
The army	belonging to	the United States.
Rules	for	conduct.
Ask a favor	from	me.
A story	about	my travels.
A man	born in	Japan.
A boy	who is	my age.

And these leave out a whole flock of other uses of *of* such as *of* course, the price *of* eggs, ten *of* five, the time *of* day, he is descended *of* kings, do it for the fun *of* it. An elementary classroom dictionary lists twenty different uses of *of*.

Among the small and troublesome words is *may*. He may go swimming. He's allowed to? There's a chance that he will?

Some ambiguities arise because of word order. Consider these three sentences:

Only he tasted the cheese.
He only tasted the cheese.
He tasted only the cheese.

(68)

The first means that he was the only one who tasted the cheese; no one else did. The second means that he merely tasted the cheese; he didn't eat a full portion. The third means that there were many items on the table, but the cheese was the only one he sampled. The headline of an advertisement for Irish International Airlines read, "And you thought Irish only flew to Ireland." What does it say? What was it meant to say?

Some of the problems in English arise from not knowing to what noun a pronoun refers. Consider this paragraph:

When Peter brought home his report card and asked his father to sign, he told him to look for his pen, which he found and brought to him. He started to sign his card, but his pen was out of ink so he brought him his pen.

Any English teacher would tell you to rewrite this, and the only way to do it would be to put in Peter's name or his father's and get rid of some of the pronouns.

The trouble here arises from the structure of Latin and other derivative languages where there are only three "persons" as the grammarians say: the first person, the speaker —I; the second person, the one spoken to—you; and the third person, the one spoken about—he, she, or it. But Algonquian languages have a finer distinction than this. There are two types of third persons. To see how this works, consider that there are two different pronouns each for *he, his,* and *him.* Let's use *he* and *hep, his* and *hisp, him* and *himp.*

The story now reads:

When Peter brought home his report card and asked his father to sign, hep told him to look for hisp pen, which he found and brought to himp. Hep started to sign his card, but hisp pen was out of ink so he brought himp his pen.

Less important, but still not to be ignored, is the part that punctuation plays in the written language. Where does the period belong here?

It was raining inside the house all the lights were on.

Does it matter whether the period goes after *raining* or after *house?*

Where do the commas belong here?

To the picnic they brought cheese bread ice cream sandwiches and soda.

How many items did they bring? Were there sandwiches or just ice cream sandwiches? Was there cheese?

Some languages, like Spanish, give you even more help, through punctuation, than English does. Spanish always signals questions and exclamations by putting the question mark and the exclamation point at the beginning of the sentence as well as at the end, so you know what to expect.

Apart from this, the rules for punctuation are pretty much the same in all languages that use the marks, and this is certainly a big help in trying to read another language. Your biggest trouble will come in trying to untangle the structure of a sentence.

So far all of the ambiguities discussed have been those that happen to be in the English language because of various accidents of its history. To concern ourselves with only such confusions is to act as if we believed that words have meanings independent of the people who speak them.

Some people do apparently believe that words have a life of their own and that it is the word, rather than what the word describes, that is most important. Have your parents or teachers insisted that you say you're sorry about something and been satisfied when you dutifully repeated, "I'm sorry"? What purpose does this serve?

When a department store sold a toy plastic truck that poured real smoke out of its exhaust pipe, parents concerned with pollution problems protested that to give children such a toy would promote the idea that air pollution is an acceptable way of life. The head of the toy company said the complaint was ridiculous. "A four-year-old child," he said, "doesn't know what the word *pollution* means."

Do words have meanings of their own? Is the meaning of a word the definition given in the dictionary, or is the dictionary simply reporting as best it can how people in general seem to use the word? Do you have normal vision? How do you know? If you do know, it's only because someone has given you an eye test. To do this it's necessary to set up some standards by which to compare your eyes with other people's. Do you have normal feelings about sunsets?

How are you going to test this? Do you have a normal understanding of the word *anger?* If people agree on the definition of a word, does it necessarily follow that they mean the same thing by it? To take a very simple example, you and I can both agree that something is *pink*. Each of us is reporting a sensation of color and we agree on the word to use for it, but are you sure that what we see is the same? If it is, how does it happen that people disagree so strongly on the question of whether certain colors clash or go well together? Would the meaning of such words as *drugs, police, war, welfare, teacher, democracy, strike* be influenced by the experience of the speaker who used the word?

One interesting way to test this question on a small scale is to play a game of word association with your friends. Provide everyone except "it" with a pencil and paper. "It" will read out a list of words and everyone is to write down very rapidly the first word that occurs to him as going with the word on the list. Start with mild, unemotional words like *chair* and move on to idea words. The words on the players' list will not be definitions, of course. Suppose, for example, you got responses like these to the word *school:*

| college | jail | dark | friends | books | arithmetic |
| principal | building | grades | job | work | ———— |

Do you have some idea of what the word *school* means to each of the players? The blank is perhaps the most interesting and revealing answer of all. How does someone feel about school if he has *no* word at hand to associate with it?

(72)

Political speakers, fund raisers, advertisers know very well that words do more than merely report actions or name objects. The words they use are designed to arouse certain associations in the minds of the hearers that will make them react in certain ways. "You've got a lot to live." What does that say? "This is the only clothes whitener that has 25 percent more bleach." This is ambiguity with a purpose.

The study of such ambiguities is an interesting one. It is the concern of semantics, a subject that can fill a book of its own.

CHAPTER VII

Sentenced to Death

So far, the discussion has been mostly of words, of how to create them, compound them, and add prefixes and suffixes, as if language were nothing but a collection of nouns and verbs and adjectives and adverbs, as if, holding a dictionary in your hand, you held the whole key to speaking, reading, and writing a language. The dictionary will give you the words, but a knowledge of the grammar of a language is what you need in order to make the dictionary work for you.

> *Before leave, will help push large box through door set shelf over desk?*

These are the basic words of a sentence, and they are in the right order, but the sentence in this form makes little sense. This is the sentence they were taken from:

> Before you leave, will you help me push a large box through the door and set it on the shelf over the desk?

(74)

There are some languages in which the sentence would be complete without putting in any of the words we first left out. The meanings of the words *will, you,* and so on would be conveyed by the use of suffixes attached to the basic words. We have some slight experience with this in English. *He did walk* means very nearly the same thing as *he walked.* In one case we used an extra word—*did*—to convey the meaning of past action. In the second case we added a suffix—*ed*—to achieve the same result. The collections of suffixes in some languages are much more elaborate than ours and serve not only to show the time of action but also to replace a large quantity of pronouns, prepositions, and conjunctions. So, to get anywhere at all with the basic words in your vocabulary, you have to know what to do with them to make a sentence out of them. What you do with them will depend on the rules of the game in the particular language you are trying to speak.

A language like Latin is very highly structured and uses verb suffixes like our *-ed* and *-ing* for every change in time of action—past, present, or future, actual or possible, continuing or completed. English needs words like *will, has, do,* and *might* as helpers. Latin almost always uses only suffixes.

A similar rule works for pronouns. To say "I go" we need two words, but in Latin the verb "go" changes according to whether it is I or you that is going. There are a few verbs in English for which this system would work. If I said simply "Am going" you would understand me without the "I" that was left out, because no other subject is possi-

(75)

ble with the verb "am." All Latin verbs are like this.

In English we say, "He gave a book *to* the boy," but Latin can do without the word "to" by changing the form of the word *boy* to include the idea of *to the*. We do this also by word order, saying *"He gave the boy a book."*

Languages like Latin, which use suffixes to replace prepositions and pronouns, are called inflecting languages. English is partly inflected: we have different forms of pronouns —though not of nouns—for subject and object. We say "She hit him," not "She hit he." Thus, even if we reversed the words and wrote "Him she hit" it would still be clear who did the hitting. But if we had the sentence "The girl hit the boy" and then reversed it in the same way—"The boy the girl hit"—it would not be possible to tell who hit whom. In Latin, or Russian, or German, you could still tell perfectly well. In some languages nouns are either male or female or neuter. In some they are all either male or female. In either case, logic has very little to do with it. In German, for example, the noun for a young girl is a neuter noun. We do some of this—but very little—in English. "Fill her up!" we say to the gas station attendant. In Italian there is no "it." Everything is male or female. In such highly inflected languages, even the adjectives change their forms to go with nouns. The endings match, so that the word for "good" is different depending upon whether it is "good boys" or "good girls" or "good milk" that is under discussion.

In the Indo-European family all languages are either highly inflected, like Latin, or partly inflected, like English and French. In these, nouns change to show singular and plural, verbs change to show past action, pronouns change to show whether they are male or female, singular or plural, subject or object. In French the adjectives also change, but, as in English, you cannot tell by looking at a noun whether it is the subject or the object. Thus word order is important, prepositions are necessary, and helping verbs are sometimes used.

Then there are languages like Chinese that are called isolating languages because each word is a separate unit. Chinese has nothing but one-syllable words—no prefixes, no suffixes, no inflections at all. Even the plural is the same as the singular, for both nouns and verbs. We have some experience with this in English with nouns like *sheep*—which may mean one or more—and with verbs like *must,* which never change. (We don't say musts, musted, musting.)

Other kinds of languages, including Hungarian, Turkish, and Finnish, have words which can be used as any part of speech—noun, verb, adjective, adverb, preposition. It is as if the word *"speech"* meant also speak, spoken, speaker, aloud, oral, and told to. These languages have no inflections except to show plural. Instead, whole words are put together. In the Ewe language of Africa, for example, there is a word that in one of its uses translates into the English verb "reach," but it can be used to mean "to." A word that in one of its uses means "come" can be used to mean "here" or "to this place," and in front of any other word used as a verb, it is the sign of the future. Thus the English sentence "I shall go to my house" would come out as "I come go reach my house."

When this method of compounding words instead of using prepositions and suffixes is taken to its furthest point, you have some of the American Indian languages like the Nootka, which was discussed in Chapter 3. In Nootka an entire sentence is made by adding word pieces together. The resulting one-word sentence cannot again be broken up into separate words.

No doubt, in your English classes year after year, a sentence was defined as a group of words expressing a complete thought. If this is the correct definition, there are some languages in which either there are no words or there are no sentences. What shall we call the Nootka version of "He invites people to a feast"? Is it a fifteen-letter word or a sentence? In any event, the rules of Latin grammar cannot be applied to it. English offers a very few examples of this where what could be a sentence on its own turns up as an adjective: "This is a *come-as-you-are* party." "This contract is offered on a *take-it-or-leave-it* basis." "He has an arrogant, *devil-may-care* attitude." But examples of this kind are limited and really do not give the flavor of such a language as Nootka because, in these examples, you can still pull the individual words out and look at them separately.

A better way to give some idea of how such a language works would be this: Think of writing English in the form of pictures such that each noun and verb has a standard picture to go with it while the connecting words—articles, prepositions, and helping verbs—are allowed to remain as words. With this rule, the sentence "The man is cutting the tree with an ax" would be written this way:

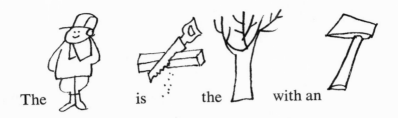

The is the with an

What the American Indian language would do with the same sentence is this:

Both pictures communicate a complete thought about equally well.

It is easy to see, through pictures, how the fusing of words takes place and how it is no longer possible to separate the individual "words" from the "sentence." It is harder to show this idea in words to someone whose language really does not permit this kind of fusing. You will have to be satisfied with the analogy.

With such a language, how do you apply the rules you have learned in school that all sentences must have a subject and a predicate? You can't. The rules apply to inflecting and partly inflecting languages like all those in the

Indo-European family, but they are by no means universal rules.

Within the Indo-European family, words can be made into sentences, the sentences do have subjects and predicates, and a noun in one language of the group will translate, if at all, into a noun in any other language of the group, a verb will translate into a verb, and so on. Thus it is easier to translate from any language of this family into another of the same family than it is to translate across family groupings.

There's no particular trick to recognizing nouns and verbs if you have been brought up to speak a language that makes a distinction between them. Professor Roger Brown, who is both a psychologist and a linguist, successfully performed an experiment like the following with four- and five-year-olds. You might try it too if you have a couple of four- or five-year-olds handy. The tests must be conducted individually and privately. Ask the first child if he knows what it means to *potch*. Then—whatever he says—show him picture number 1 and say, "Here is a picture of *potching*."

Then show him pictures 2 and 3 and ask, "Can you show me another picture of potching?"

Move then to pictures 4, 5, and 6. Ask the child if he has ever seen any *vorp*. Show him picture 4 and say, "There is some *vorp* in this picture. Can you see it? Can you find another picture [showing him 5 and 6] with some *vorp* in it?"

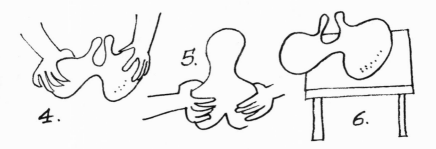

Reverse your tests with the second child. For pictures 1, 2, and 3 say, "Have you ever seen any *potch?* There is some *potch* in this picture," and continue with the questions. For pictures 4, 5, and 6 ask for a picture of *vorping*.

You will probably find that your subjects can correctly identify the motion as the verb, the substance as the noun. Two-thirds of Professor Brown's subjects passed, although his tests were harder, requiring the children to identify a container (a *vorp,* for instance) with some *potch* (a mass noun) in it, as well as the motion of *potching* or *vorping*.

Do you remember "Jabberwocky" from Lewis Carroll's *Through the Looking-Glass*?

'Twas brillig, and the slithy toves
Did gyre and gimble in the wabe;
All mimsy were the borogoves
And the mome raths outgrabe.

The words are those of some unknown splandrumpchifying language, but the grammar is pure English. Isn't it child's play to pick out the nouns, verbs, and adjectives?

What is the advantage of being able to distinguish nouns from verbs? If you want to translate from one language to another, knowing how a word is used saves a lot of time and prevents you from making a fool of yourself. Suppose the sentence you would like to translate into German is "I want to train my dog." The question is what is the German word for *train?* You're using *train* as a verb; therefore you can ignore all the noun meanings of *train* you find in your English-German dictionary. You will not get bogged down in the train that sweeps behind the lady's gown, or caught up in the wheels of the railroad train.

Even when looking up unfamiliar words in your own language, if you stop to consider how the word is used in the sentence that gives you trouble, to decide that it is used as a noun, when you get to the dictionary and find half a column of suggested uses, you can skip all the ones that are clearly irrelevant by going directly to the group that are used as nouns.

You must also make yourself aware of which words in English are purely a matter of grammar and have no meaning on their own. They are like silent consonants in spelling, which would make hash of the word if you tried to pronounce them, as if you said *for-e-ig-ner*. Suppose, for example, you want to translate "Are there any good restaurants nearby?" If you look for a translation for *there* you will find a word that means the opposite of *here*. Will it be useful? *There* in that sentence doesn't mean anything, and not all other languages have this grammatical peculiarity. The sentence is exactly equivalent to "Are any good restaurants nearby?" and this sentence *is* translatable. *Do* is another such meaningless word when it is used as the first word in a question. "Do you like milk" translates into other languages as "You like milk?" or "Like you milk?"

Do other languages have such pieces of extra baggage as *do* and *there?* Of course. If you've been scolded for saying "I don't know nothing" or "I won't tell nobody" because the double negative is unnecessary, you'll be happy to know that this is the *right* way to say it in French or Spanish.

One tricky aspect of learning a foreign language is that it is easy to be insulting without meaning to. Many languages have two different words for "you." One is used to intimate friends, to children, pets, and servants. The other is used in formal conversation, in talking with people you don't know well, with your elders and your superiors. (It is something like the question of calling somebody by his first name, but not quite.) To use the intimate form to a person you don't know well may easily offend him, as if you called to a

(83)

grown man, "Hey, boy!" This is why many conversational language courses in French, Spanish, and German do not teach the intimate form of the pronoun and the verbs that go with it. But what does that do to the romance you're trying to have on your trip abroad? Imagine a date during which you call each other Miss and Mister all evening long!

The problems of translation, then, are not so much a question of what the words mean, as of how to use them. As one visiting professor from Germany, struggling to lecture in English, phrased it, "We will now overlook" the problems of word order.

Of all the differences among Indo-European languages, word order causes the most confusion because, although the basic sentence structure is the same, the rules for word order vary widely. There are many exceptions like "Came the dawn" or like the electric company's apologetic sign "Dig we must," but the general rule in English is that the subject comes before the main verb, and the direct object, if there is one, comes third. Adjectives come in front of the nouns they describe. These rules are not the same in other languages. In French the adjective sometimes comes ahead of the noun, but mostly it comes after—"a street empty," not "an empty street." In German, the adjective comes ahead of the noun, but if there are any helping verbs in the sentence, the main verb always comes last. Objects come either in the middle or at the beginning of the sentence. "Why can I the book not in the pocket put?" is very poor English, but it is excellent German. So is "Evenings will we then together in theater go."

Mark Twain enjoyed himself writing English as if it were German. Here is one of his most famous pieces:

I might gladly the separable verb also a little bit reform. I might none let do what Schiller did: he has the whole history of the Thirty Years' War between the two members of a separate verb in-pushed. That has even Germany itself aroused, and one has Schiller the permission refused the History of the Hundred Years' War to compose—God be it thanked!

Remember the trouble that English had in fitting its sounds into the Latin alphabet? It has the same trouble fitting its rules of grammar into those of Latin grammar. The Latin alphabet was the one that was available, like it or not, and the Latin grammar was imposed upon English by the grammarians, who were all Latin scholars. They thought of Latin as the perfect language from which other languages unfortunately had deteriorated. The early grammarians then did not see themselves as reporters describing how the language was in fact put together and spoken by its native speakers. Rather they saw themselves as rulemakers who had the right to tell people how they should speak and write their language. Any deviation from this that the grammarians could not "correct" they noted as exceptions to the rule. The early linguists took this attitude with them in analyzing languages outside the Indo-European group as well and, had they met Nootka, they would actually have attempted to discover and single out the subject and predicate of a Nootka sentence.

(85)

They would have been astonished to discover that there are some languages even more highly inflected in some cases than Latin. In Latin—and in English—one says, "When I was five years old, I went to school for the first time" as if the "I" that went to school at the age of five and the "I" that is telling the story are one unchanging person. Are you the same person you were at the age of five? Mende, a Sudanese African language, thinks not. In Mende it is pronouns rather than verbs that are inflected to show tense, that is, time of occurrence. In some languages such as Hebrew, not only adjectives but even verbs are inflected to show whether it is a man or a woman that is performing the act.

Because the grammarians were so bound up in Latin grammar, they insisted on finding inflections in English where there were none. They set forth in the grammar books so-called conjugations of English verbs, trying to make them look like Latin. This is the grammarians' table, matching the English verb with the Latin:

Present Tense

	Singular		Plural	
1st person	I love	amo	we love	amamus
2nd person	you love	amas	you love	amatis
3rd person	he, she, or it loves	amat	they love	amant

This is all very well, but anyone looking straight at the English (and not through the spectacles of Latin) will see that there are only two forms for *love* in the present tense—*love* and *loves*—and in the past tense there's only one—*loved* —no matter what pronoun goes with it.

The only remaining trace of a Latin type of inflection in English is the insistence that the verb match the subject for singular or plural use in the present tense. Some pronouns are inflected as well to show whether they are used as subject or object, but some—*you* and *it*—are not. English also insists that the pronouns *he, she,* and *it* be used properly with the nouns they stand for, so that we do not say, "I saw the girl and I gave it the book" when we mean that the book was given to her. This may seem to you to be an obvious necessity but it is not. German uses the same word— *sie*—to stand for *she, you,* and *they.* Hungarian gets along with only one word for *he, she,* and *it.* If this is surprising, ask yourself what the plural forms are, in English, for *he, she,* and *it. They* does the work for all three.

Sometimes the rule for agreement of subject and verb involves one in silly predicaments. You could explain that there are two kinds of pronouns—those that use the same verb as the noun they stand for (for example: John works and he works), and those that don't (for example: John works and you work—if your name is John). Under this rule *"You* is a pronoun with which you can't use *is."* But of course, I just did, correctly.

The insistence of the grammarians that every sentence must have a subject and a predicate—as I'm sure you've been told, year in and year out—leads to some very artificial kinds of reasoning. The subject, they say, is what the sentence is about, or "who did it?" while the predicate describes the action that the subject did or had done to it. Fine with sentences like "The cat ate the mouse" or "The mouse was eaten by the cat." But what about sentences like "It never rains but it pours"? *It* is the subject. It's a pronoun referring to something. To what? What is the "it" that rains? If you say that "it" means the rain, then the rain never rains but the rain pours. Accepted. Now tell me, what else besides rain rains? Does this sentence *really* have both a subject and a verb? Or is the Hopi language more logical when it regards this sentence as having no nouns or pronouns, but only verbs?

What is the subject of the sentence "Get out!"? The grammarians will tell you that it is "you, understood," but that's only because the grammarians have already ruled that every sentence has got to have a subject. "Beautiful day!" you say to your friend. "That's not a sentence," say the grammarians, "because it has neither subject nor verb. You should say, 'It is a beautiful day' or 'The day is beautiful.'" Do these convey different meanings?

What will the grammarians do with languages like Hebrew, Russian, Chinese, and Malay, which get along very well without the verb *is,* saying simply, "Day beautiful"? If no one stops them, they'll tell you that *is* is "understood"— even in a language that has no word *is* to "understand."

Grammarians try very hard to exert their authority to keep the language pure and correct, and this is generally a good thing to try to do. But sometimes they are a bit like King Canute, who sat on the shore, according to legend, and commanded the waves to come no closer. The grammar of a language is no more static—unchanging—than the meaning of words. In the nineteenth century, grammarians were deeply concerned that the language was being ruined. People were saying "The bridge is being built" instead of "The bridge is building," which grammarians said was the only correct way. (We still use the old form in "The eggs are boiling.") Somehow the English language has survived this ruination, as it will doubtless survive "It's me" and "Who are you talking about?"

As to the rules about not ending sentences with prepositions, the neatest comment was made by Winston Churchill when he said, "This is the kind of English up with which I will not put."

There's a great deal of emphasis in English classes on the question of whether something is an adjective or an adverb. His writing is *clear* because he writes *clearly*. "But," you protest, "he has a fast car and it goes fast." That does not faze the grammarians. Fast, they say, is both an adjective and an adverb. What part of speech is *easy* in the sentence "go easy"? The dictionary will tell you that *easy* is an adverb meaning *easily*. Is it? How about *right* in "Do it right?" Grammarians can argue for hours about how to diagram the sentence "Paint the town red." The more learned among them will come up with the solution that the sentence is an abbreviated form of "Paint the town to be red" because that can be diagrammed. Isn't it just as logical to say that "go easy" means "go in such a way as to be easy" and "do it right" is "do it in such a way as to make it right"? And is all this beating around the bush really necessary?

I'm sure you've been told time and time again that there are four kinds of sentences—statements, questions, exclamations, and commands, and that the first two are the most important to distinguish. "Isn't it a beautiful day?" Is that really a question? The grammarians' logic can't untangle a sentence like "You are going, aren't you?"

But let's not abolish the grammarians. A total absence of standards would make for chaos, and a total ignorance of the rules would blur the lines of communication quite badly. We no longer wear the costumes of the nineteenth century, but neither do we go naked. There must be rules, and people must know what they are, but they must not be thought so sacred that any change is treason, nor so perfect that any language that does not follow them is somehow inferior. If you learn the rules of your own language, you will find it easier to learn other languages, especially the highly structured ones, because you have something to compare. But at the point where you think your own language has the most logical—if not the only—way to put words together, you are in trouble.

CHAPTER VIII

Me Is Who, Who Is He, He Is She

The chapter heading is a phrase I learned in childhood when I was studying Hebrew. It was supposed to be helpful in memorizing Hebrew words. *Me* is the sound of the Hebrew word for "who"; *hoo* is the sound of the Hebrew word for "he"; and *he* is the sound of the Hebrew word for "she." Nobody is asking you to keep this straight because any time you really need to know this, it's easy to look it up. For words alone, you can use a dictionary, but unfortunately the dictionary will not tell you that to ask "Who is he?" in Hebrew you would have to find the words for "Who he this?"

Words that are simply the names of common objects and actions are fairly easy for an English-speaking person to come by in any European language of the Indo-European family, because English has the great advantage of mixed parentage—Latin and Germanic—and therefore shares the roots of words with many other languages. Those that stem from Latin—French, Italian, Spanish, and Portuguese—are easier to understand when you read them than when you hear them spoken because, as you saw with the word *Paris* (*pah-ree'*) the spelling is often the same, but the pronunciation may be so different as to convey nothing to your ear. You already have a reading knowledge of several hundred words in these languages. To prove it, here's a small list—fifteen words in each of four languages—that you can read. The words all mean exactly what you think they do:

French	Spanish	Portuguese	Italian
air	aire	ar	aria
caverne	cueva	caverna	caverna
désert	desierto	deserto	deserto
muscle	músculo	musculo	muscolo
animal	animal	animal	animale
éléphant	elefante	elefante	elefante
hôpital	hospital	hospital	ospedale
acteur	actor	actor	attore
docteur	doctor	doutor	dottore
dentiste	dentista	dentista	dentista
distance	distancia	distância	distanza
instrument	instrumento	instrumento	strumento
problème	problema	problema	problema
système	sistema	sistema	sistema
minute	minuto	minuto	minuto

What a painless way to learn fifteen words in each of four languages! Notice also how easy it would be for the speakers of any of these languages to learn any of the others—as far as words alone are concerned. They would have trouble with most of the words in the next group of languages, but you will not:

Swedish	Danish	Dutch	German
natur	natur	natuur	natur
vind	vind	wind	wind
arm	arm	arm	arm
finger	finger	vinger	finger
hand	haand	hand	hand
bank	bank	bank	bank
adress	adresse	adres	adresse
sekund	sekund	seconde	sekunde
fast	fast	vast	fest
dum	dum	dum	dom
giva	give	geven	geben
hava	have	hebben	haben
landa	lande	landen	landen
stinka	stinke	stinken	stinken
hatt	hat	hoed	hut

Some of these would be unfamiliar if you heard them. The German *wind,* for example, is pronounced "vint" and *stinken* is "shtinken," but once you learned a few simple rules about the change in consonants—both in sound and spelling—from early roots, not only would these words be understood but so would many others. *Better* turns into German *besser; water* becomes *wasser,* and every such word with a *t* sound in the center turns up with an *s* sound.

Words in English that begin with *th* begin with a *d* in German: *thick* is *dick, thing* is *ding,* and so on.

Be careful, though, of deciding that you can tell what all foreign words mean by looking at them. There are some serious exceptions: *pain* means "bread" in French; *gift* means "poison" in German, for example.

Some words are the same in languages all over the world not because the languages stem from a common parent but because the things they name are of recent discovery or invention and often, though not always, the name travels with the invention. Some examples are *restaurant, automobile, aspirin,* and *telephone.* (The spelling may vary to conform with the spelling rules of the language.) Not all languages do this, however. German, instead of accepting the word *telephone,* took the two parts of the word, *tele*("far") and *phone*("sound") and translated them into German, getting *fernspreche*—"far-speak."

How do you go about finding the meaning of a word you want in a foreign language? If the word is something like *bread* or *milk* or *horse,* the dictionary will give you a ready answer, because these words have one meaning only in any language (apart from slang, of course). But suppose you want to look up a word like *right.* You'll find a dozen translations for it, and how will you choose the one that's appropriate? Try to think of an English synonym for *right* as you propose to use it. *Correct,* for example? Then look up *correct* as well. If you find the same word given in the definitions for both *correct* and *right,* you'll know you're safe. Suppose the sentence that you want to translate is "I'll do it

(94)

right away." Will it help you to look up *right?* If, as a foreigner, you looked up *right* and *away* in the dictionary, would you be able to discover the meaning of the sentence?

Right away is an idiom—a phrase you can't make sense of by finding the meanings of the separate words in it. All languages have idioms, and idioms always cause trouble to students of the language. The first step, then, in translating a sentence like "I'll do it right away" from English to another language is to translate it from English to English until you have a word or a phrase whose meaning is not ambiguous. "I'll do it immediately" is a substitute that can be translated. Can you put the following idioms into translatable English?

He gets on my nerves.
I can't make head or tail of what he says.
Do they hit it off?
Keep in touch with me.
Who's going to look after the animals while we're gone?
Let's make for home.
He passed out from the heat.
Please see about getting tickets.
I won't stand for that.
I took it for granted that he would come.
It's up to you to decide.
I won't put up with your behavior.
Don't let on that you know.
Don't give in.
Do you go in for swimming?
How's he getting on?

Along with the idioms of a language that make translation difficult is the poetry of the language. Not just poems, but the poetry that is built right into the language we speak every day. It is full of metaphor—comparing something to something else without actually saying you're doing that. Consider the *elbow* of a pipe, the *foot* of a mountain, the *lip* of a pot, a plumber's *snake,* all perfectly ordinary phrases in common use, but whoever first thought them up was something of a poet. Are these images necessarily the same in all languages? No, in English we speak of the *bridge* of the nose, but to a Spaniard it resembles the ridge of a roof and that is his term for it.

Some of the metaphors in our speech have been there for so long that the imagery may entirely escape us. Think of what's behind the phrase "a *coat* of paint," "the *eye* of a hurricane," "a *blanket* of clouds," "a *branch* of learning," or "the *star* of a show."

We apply the names of parts of the body to tools and machines, so that a clock has a *face* and *hands,* a bell has a *tongue,* tables and chairs have *legs,* hammers have *heads,* and record players have tone *arms.* We compare the structure of people and animals to buildings. Houses have *wings* and mouths have *roofs.* A stairway has a *foot* and a foot has an *arch.*

Other languages have equally poetic but different images. German calls a thimble a *finger-hat;* it calls a glove a *hand-shoe.* But it is no more likely that the Germans who use these terms think of thimbles as hats for fingers than that we think of the feet of wild creatures when we mention the *claw* of a hammer. These poetic terms have worked their way so deeply into the language that they no longer call forth the images that originally created them. Uncle George is *eccentric* and so is a wheel: they're both "off center." We think nothing of the term *"shoulder* of the road"—at least not until we come to a sign "SOFT SHOULDERS" and find it amusing. We don't think about the *"eye* of a potato" until a young child asks why a potato has more eyes than he does and whether it can see behind it. We *pinpoint* a problem or we *highlight* it, we *spearhead* a campaign and we build a strong *framework* for an argument, and all without thinking of pins or lights, of spears or the construction of a building.

All of these are words that will be tricky when you look them up in a foreign language. But it is in any event a good idea to become aware of the images behind the metaphors in your language. When you are not, some strange mixtures can occur: "If you play your cards right, you'll hit the bull's eye." (In what strange game could that occur?) "There's a bottleneck in the production line that will have to be ironed out." (What will it look like then?) Will the labor organizer "raise the roof" if the "ceiling on wages is lowered"? Can you "weigh an opinion carefully to see if it will hold water"?

Interesting problems arise for translators in deciding how to translate a metaphor. Shall the translator try to preserve the imagery or shall he try to convey its straightforward intended meaning? "To hit the nail on the head" for an American is to be exactly right, but the same phrase to a Spaniard means "to strike it rich." Suppose in a

Spanish story a boy was accused of looking at his notes during a test and he denied it. Would you know what was meant when the story went on to say he "was caught with the chicken under his arm"? If you were doing a written translation of the story for other Americans to read, would you write it that way, or would you say that he "was caught red-handed"?

The poetic aspects of a language are hard enough to deal with, but the poetry itself presents a far more difficult problem to the translator. The images in a poem are the new creations of the poet, not those that are already embedded in the language. Shall a translator try to convey into another language exactly the image the poet had in mind, or shall he substitute an image that will arouse the same feelings in the readers of the translation? What would "as sultry as a February afternoon" mean to you? It could be a translation of a line from an Argentine poet's work, for, in Argentina, in the southern hemisphere, seasons are the reverse of ours. Should the translator change it to July? Poetry seldom carries footnotes.

Poetry that has rhyme and rhythm is even harder to deal with. The translator almost always has to decide whether to preserve the rhyme or the image. In English, *night* rhymes with *light,* and these words are frequently rhymed in English poems. But in French the word for *night—nuit—* rhymes with the word for *noise—bruit* (pronounced *nwee* and *brwee*). The word for *light* rhymes with *air*. Obviously the translator has a problem. Even where the words in two languages are identical, the pronunciation, particularly the accented syllable, may make them utterly different. *Paris* in English rhymes with *embarrass,* but in French it rhymes with *Marie.* What does this do to the rhythm of a poem?

This is one of the main reasons why people want to learn foreign languages. The literature of a language is closed to you, as literature, unless you can read it for yourself in the language in which it was written, after you have learned the language well enough to think in it. As long as you are reaching for a dictionary to translate word by word or trying to remember facts like "me is who and who is he," all the poems that have been written in the world are lost to you unless they happen to have been written in English.

Not only poems, but also many jokes are lost because they depend on a play on words. In translation they are meaningless. Every language also has some words that are not translatable into other languages except by long explanations that do not fit well into poetry or jokes. You have really learned another language not just when you can give an English word for every word in the language that you know, but rather when you stop and say, "I can't translate that; there is no English word for that" and yet you know what it means.

CHAPTER IX

Bricks from the Tower of Babel

According to the Bible story, there was a time when "the whole earth was of one language and of one speech." But when it occurred to the people to build a tower that would reach unto Heaven itself, the Lord was angry and said, "Let us go down, and there confound their language that they may not understand one another's speech." And the building was stopped and the men scattered because they could no longer understand one another.

Is it possible that the people of the world today could agree upon a single international language that everyone would be able to speak and understand? This has been the dream of many linguists over the centuries, and almost a thousand languages have been invented for this purpose, not to replace the native languages but to provide a second language for worldwide communication.

For about a thousand years—from about the fifth century through the fifteenth—Latin was the second language of educated people all over Europe and all scholarly works were written in Latin. For, before the invention of the printing press, reading and writing were skills known only to scholars. Most of the scholars were priests and clergymen, and Latin was the language of the Church. Latin was a subject required in schools and in colleges, and all educated people had some familiarity with it.

The number of people who study Latin has not grown smaller, but proportionately it has become very much smaller. As ordinary men all over the world began to be able to read and write their own languages, and as scientific work of the sixteenth and later centuries came more and more to be written in living languages, a knowledge of Latin was not so essential. Thus, although Latin might once have been claimed as the most suitable of international languages (at least for Europeans), this time has passed.

The earliest attempts to invent a simplified language for international use came in the seventeenth century, but it was not until the late nineteenth century that any sizable group of people did actually attempt to speak and write an artificial language. Esperanto, which was published in 1887, was the first language really to take hold. At one time or another as many as eight million people have learned Esperanto. It has been taught in a great many schools and colleges in Europe, and the study of Esperanto was even made compulsory in some high schools in Germany.

Five-sixths of Esperanto words have Latin roots; the remainder are Germanic. Verbs are still inflected for tense, and nouns have separate forms for use as subject and object in a sentence.

Ido and Interlingua followed Esperanto and improved it, by cutting out some of the cumbersome Latin grammar that still remained.

In 1928, Otto Jesperson, the famous Danish linguist who is known as the greatest authority on the English language, put forth a concoction of his own called Novial. It was an improvement on Esperanto but still had the same basic approach. Jesperson thought that the best type of international language was one that offered the greatest ease of learning to the greatest number of people. His, therefore, included more Germanic roots and leaned more heavily on the structure of English than on Latin. But when Jesperson thinks of the "greatest number of people" he is referring to Europeans or people of other continents whose language and culture derives from Europe. This completely excludes native populations of the continents of Asia and Africa and of the Pacific Islands, for whom Novial would be totally unfamiliar.

How easy is it going to be for someone in whose language *me* is who, *who* is he, and *he* is she to learn an international language based on Latin roots?

Still, if the language is a well-constructed one and not too complicated, perhaps it could nevertheless be adopted by those unfamiliar with its roots and structure.

What kind of problem does the linguist face in inventing a language? What are the essentials of a language? What must he keep and what may he discard to simplify the language for people trying to learn it? For one thing, he can remove all the exceptions to rules. Whatever rules there are for spelling, pronunciation, and usage can be uniformly applied. What about inflection? Is it necessary to have separate forms for singular and plural? Is it necessary to have some sort of suffix like -ed to indicate past tense? Consider this pair of sentences and decide which is clearer:

I cut the wool of two sheep yesterday.
I sheared two goats yesterday.

They're equally good, aren't they, although the word *cut* is the same in the present and past. No suffix has been added, but the word *yesterday* makes it clear that the action is in the past. The word *two* makes it perfectly obvious that the sheep are just as plural as the goats, without the addition of an -s.

Consider these two sentences:

I told you about it.
I told him about her.

Are they equally clear? Yet *it* and *you* have the same form when they are objects as when they are subjects. It seems that inflection of pronouns could be discarded in creating an international language. Interglossa, the most recent of the proposed artificial languages, takes these reforms into account and, in addition, uses basically the Chinese structure, which is that of an isolating language where each word stands alone and there are no inflections at all. The

(103)

rules of grammar in Interglossa are largely rules of word order, as in English and more strictly in Chinese. The roots are basically Latin and Greek because these have been the roots of most scientific words and are therefore—to some extent—familiar to scientists all over the world.

The use of Latin and Greek roots is a big help to readers of Indo-European languages because it enables them to spot on sight words that are like their own. This is where some of the apparent deadweight of English spelling comes in handy. Words beginning with *ps,* for example, signal their Greek origin. Because *debt* and *doubt* are spelled as they are, with that absurd silent *b,* we can not only recognize their relationship to *debit* for the first and *dubious* for the second but can also see their connection with the Latin words *debitum,* "a debt," and *dubito,* "I doubt." The words in Interglossa are equally easy to spot. While this is of no help to the people who speak non-Indo-European languages, the use of Latin roots has at least the advantage of straightforward rules for spelling and pronunciation. The Latin alphabet was, after all, designed for writing Latin, and all the sounds of Latin are represented by its letters. There are no problems of *th* and *ch* and so on to deal with. (Incidentally, if you never solved the spelling puzzles of Chapter V, the answers are ei*ghth,* gli*mps*ing, and mean*wh*ile.)

Why must an international language necessarily be a made-up language? Why can't one of the existing languages be chosen as the best one to try to internationalize? In the United Nations, for example, there are five official languages—English, Chinese, Russian, French, and Spanish—and at all official meetings simultaneous translation is carried on, so that it is possible to listen to the speeches in any one of the five languages. If a delegate does not know at least one of these languages, he must learn one. How about making one of these into an international language? Of these, Chinese and Russian are not likely to gain many supporters because of the difficulties of their alphabets. The Russian alphabet stems from the Greek but is like that of very few other languages in the world today. The Chinese alphabet is not an alphabet at all. Its characters represent ideas, not sounds, and would therefore require someone to learn two separate languages—the written and the spoken. The fact that Chinese characters are associated with idea, not sound, would make it a fine *written* international language, since each reader could apply the symbol to the appropriate word in his own language.

French was once the language of international diplomats, and a great many people involved in international relations had to learn French and did. But it has never been a language of science. Its spelling is difficult for foreigners and some of the sounds in French, being unlike those of other Latin-based languages, are hard for non-Frenchmen to master.

Spanish comes off well in both spelling and pronunciation, for its rules are simple and there are almost no exceptions to these rules, but it is highly inflected and even adds such complications as having two different forms for the verb *to be,* depending upon whether the state of being is permanent or temporary. In simplified form, it might do very well, but no one has tried to promote Spanish as the international language.

English, on the other hand, has been worked on for this purpose. C. K. Ogden and I. A. Richards, who are most famous for their book on logic *The Meaning of Meaning,* set themselves the task of discovering what is the smallest number of words we need to have in order to be able to define all of the other words in English. They came up with the answer of eight hundred and fifty and made a basic word list of eight hundred and fifty English words, which they named Basic English. These are the only verbs in the entire list:

come	go	get	give	keep	let
make	put	seem	take	be	do
have	say	see	send	may	will

With these go the rules for adding *-ing* and *-ed* and for the irregular changes like come-came-come. All the parts of the verb *to be*—*is, are, were,* and so on—are considered as the one word *be.*

The verbs are listed as "operations" and are coupled with eighty-two other words—prepositions, pronouns, conjunctions, and adverbs.

To transform these words into other familiar verbs in English, one learns to put two operations together. Thus "to depart" is to *go away,* "to follow" is to *go after,* "to return" is to *go again,* "to attack" is to *go against.* With the verb *to make* you can produce such combinations as *make clean, make wet, make ready, make well,* and *make trouble.*

A great many other verb ideas are available from the list of four hundred things and one hundred and fifty qualities, many of which can be used with the rule that you may add *-ing* and *-ed* to them. Thus while, strictly speaking, there is no verb *to protest* in Basic English, you can say either "I make a protest" or "I am a protesting man."

Writing in Basic English may require you to use a greater number of words—as in having to say "it came to my ears" instead of "I heard"—but you can still say anything you want to with just 850 *different* words and a few suffixes: *-ed, -ing, -ly,* and the prefixes *in-* and *un-* for "not." This is a much smaller number of words to have to memorize than is ordinarily offered to the student of a foreign language.

The trouble with learning Basic, though, is that while you do not have to learn a large vocabulary, you do have to learn a great number of idioms. Someone who already knows English will have no trouble with Basic, of course. But will it be readily understood by someone who does not know English that *go with* means "be suitable," that *put up with* means "endure"? How is a foreigner to know that you *put* a question to someone rather than *give* a question to him, or that "I had a good mind to make it" means "I intended to make it?" The vocabulary of Basic is simple to learn, but the way words are put together is not.

The problem of translating from one language to another is far less likely to be that of not knowing the right word than of not knowing where to put it in the sentence or what other words it can be teamed up with. So it is questionable whether it is easier to learn a long word list or to learn a great many unfamiliar combinations like *make out, make little of, put up with.*

Basic English and most of the other languages that have been proposed as international languages have one great disability for their acceptance as a world language: they all assume that the structure of Indo-European languages is generally understood worldwide. (Interglossa is the only important exception, as it makes the attempt to use Chinese isolating structure instead.) As Benjamin Whorf, the expert on American Indian languages pointed out, "We say 'a large black and white hunting dog' and assume that in Basic English one would do the same. How is the speaker of a radically different mother tongue supposed to know that he cannot say 'hunting white black large dog'?"

Finally, in considering the merits of any proposed international language it's important to remember what it can and cannot be expected to do. If it is to be used for anything other than basic understanding between people of different nationalities in their daily lives, in international affairs, and in the exchange of scientific information, all proposals are likely to be rejected. If you think of it as a way of internationalizing literature—especially poetry—forget it. Admittedly, translations of the Gettysburg Address, of *Treasure Island, Black Beauty,* and other books of fiction into Basic English came out remarkably well, but no one who could read the original would accept the Basic English version instead.

In a translation into Basic English of a play by George

Bernard Shaw, "an old soldier" turns into *a man who has been in the army a long time*. Here are three lines from the play to compare:

Shaw	Basic
You will shoot me. How do you know that I am afraid to die?	You will let off your gun at me. Why are you so certain that I have a fear of death?
I couldn't believe my eyes.	I simply had no belief in my eyes.
That is to say, he was a pretender and a coward! You did not dare to say that before.	That is to say, he was not what he seemed, and was in fact in fear of danger! You had not the face to say that before.

Is it possible to say everything you need to say in Basic English or Esperanto or any of the other artificial international languages? The answer depends upon what you mean by "need."

What do you *need* to eat? Good, body-building food? Then why do we need Hungarian goulash, shish kebab, sauerbraten, chili con carne? What's a five-hundred-page cookbook for? Why doesn't everyone cook food in some simple, nourishing, tasteful, agreed-upon way? What's wrong with hamburger?

An artificial language is a kind of worldwide hamburger. Or perhaps it's a uniform. Uniforms are usually well-designed, comfortable, protective clothing, a great deal more practical and useful than the sometimes flimsy, sometimes cumbersome clothing people choose to wear.

If language were for nothing but the communication of warnings and weather reports, an artificial international language would do nicely. But man has always had a need to do more than simply "tell it like it is." His language is for reporting not merely his work but how he feels about his work. In his language he defines himself. For this, a language needs idiom, needs all the oddities of grammar and style that reflect its history and development, all the poetic turns of phrase that have enriched it over the centuries. The language *needs* these? Well, perhaps not. Does a man *need* eyebrows? If you were to construct a man, would you give him eyebrows? Is there some special reason why his lips should be a different color from the rest of his face? Perhaps not, but this is how people—real people—are.

Artificial language is recommended highly for artificial man. The computers need it and hopefully will find it to simplify communication among themselves. For communication between men, languages in all their diversity will remain and grow as mirrors of the growth and soul of the societies that speak them.

WHERE TO GO FROM HERE

There are a great many books dealing with the origin of language in general or with that of particular words. A few of these are listed below. If you cannot find these particular titles in your school or public library, there will doubtless be others on the shelves numbered 400–412 in the Dewey Decimal System.

These are books about language in general, the history of the English language and comparison of English with other languages:

Epstein, Sam and Beryl. *First Book of Words.* New York: Franklin Watts, Inc., 1954.

Laird, Helene and Charlton. *The Tree of Language.* New York and Cleveland: World Publishing Co., 1958.

Ludovici, L. J. *Origins of Language.* New York: G. P. Putnam's Sons, 1965.

Pei, Mario. *All About Language.* Philadelphia: J. B. Lippincott Co., 1954.

Sparks, William. *The Making of Linguistics.* New York: Abelard-Schuman, 1969.

These books are more concerned with the origin of particular words:

Asimov, Isaac. *Words from History.* New York: Houghton Mifflin, 1969.

Epstein, Sam and Beryl. *What's Behind the Word.* New York: Scholastic Book Services (paperback), 1964.

Lambert, Eloise. *Our Language—The Story of the Words We Use.* New York: Lothrop, Lee & Shepard Co., Inc., 1955.

Longman, Harold. *What's Behind the Word?* New York: Coward McCann, 1968.

Nurnberg, Maxwell. *Wonders in Words.* Englewood Cliffs, N.J.: Prentice-Hall, Inc., 1969.

Finally, there are books dealing with written language, from ancient cuneiform stonecutting to the language of computers today. Two of these are:

Cahn, William and Rhoda. *The Story of Writing.* New York: Harvey House, Inc., 1963.

Gordon, Keith. *The Romance of Writing.* New York: The Viking Press, 1956.

INDEX

German language, 39, 50, 65, 76, 84-85, 91, 93-94, 96
    compared with other languages, 24
Germanic group languages, 24-25, 30-31, 101, 102
Gh (sound), 36, 59-60
Grammar, 74-90
    adjectives, 78, 86, 89-90
    adverbs, 89-90
    compound words, 77-79
    inflections, 75-77, 79-80, 86-87
    Latin, 85-86
    nouns, 76-77, 80-90
    objects, 76-77, 84
    predicates, 79-80, 87-88
    prepositions, 76, 77, 89
    pronouns, 75-77, 83-84, 86-87
    punctuation, 70-71
    singular and plural nouns, 77, 103
    subjects, 76-77, 79-80, 87-88
    suffixes, 75-76
    verbs, 74-76, 77, 80-90, 103
    See also Words
Grammarians, 85, 86, 88-90
Greek language, 25, 36, 104

Hamito-Semitic group languages, 30-31
Hebrew language, 48-49, 86, 88, 91
    compared with other languages, 30-31
Helping verbs, 75, 77
Heraclitus, 16-17
Heredity, 11-12

Hopi language, 88
Hungarian language, 77

Idioms
    Basic English and, 107
    translation of, 95
Ido language, 102
Imagery, 96-98
-in prefix, 55, 107
Indian languages. *See* American Indian languages
Indo-Chinese group languages, 30
Indo-European languages, 26, 27-31, 91
    inflection of, 76-77, 79-80, 86-87
    prefixes, 47-48
    root words, 26, 35, 47-48, 64, 65, 104
    suffixes, 47-48
    See also names of languages
Inflecting languages, 47-49, 76-77, 79-80, 86-87
-ing suffixes, 47, 75, 106, 107
Interglossa, 103-104, 108
Interlingua, 102
International languages, 100-110
    Basic English, 106-109
    disadvantages of, 109-110
    Esperanto, 101-102
    idioms and, 107
    Ido, 102
    Interglossa, 103-104, 108
    Interlingua, 102
    Novial, 102
Isolating languages, 77
Italian language, 92
    compared with other languages, 22-23, 25

About the Author

Jessica Davidson received a B.A. from the University of Wisconsin, an M.S. from Danbury State College and a law degree from Columbia University. She served as an opinions attorney with the U.S. Department of Labor and later became a teacher in the Newtown, Connecticut public schools.

Ms. Davidson traces her interest in language back to her childhood when her father, in order to stem her flow of words, told her of the old legend that each child is issued at birth a given quota of words to speak. When those words are used up, then life ends. Since one can never discover how many words one has been allotted, prudence dictates a careful selection and sparing use. She noted, however, that nothing was ever mentioned in the legend about the *written* word . . .

The author's previous books include a text for teachers entitled *Using Cuisenaire Rods,* a puzzle book called *Mind in a Maze,* a book on logic called *The Square Root of Tuesday,* and *What I Tell You Three Times is True,* which is about semantics.